D1795681

THE CLEVELAND
STREET AFFAIR

THE CLEVELAND STREET AFFAIR

Lewis Chester
David Leitch
Colin Simpson

WEIDENFELD AND NICOLSON
LONDON

Copyright © 1976 by Lewis A Chester,
David Leitch, and C. and J. Simpson Ltd.

First published in Great Britain in 1977 by
Weidenfeld and Nicolson 11 St John's Hill
London SW 11

All rights reserved. No part of this
publication may be reproduced, stored in
a retrieval system, or transmitted, in
any form or by any means, electronic,
mechanical, photocopying, recording or
otherwise, without the prior permission
of the copyright owner.

ISBN 0 297 77113 2

Printed in Great Britain by
REDWOOD BURN LIMITED
Trowbridge & Esher

Acknowledgments

The Keeper of the Rolls Room at the Public Records Office, London, together with his staff and photocopying assistants were a great help to us, as were the librarians of the London Library, Camden, Westminster, Croydon, Surrey County Council and the New York Public Libraries. We are also grateful to the staff of the British Museum Reading Room, Manuscripts Room, Newspaper and North Libraries. Miss Penny Brown researched the illustrations and the indefatigable Miss Ann Rye typed the manuscript.

Acknowledgeme...

Contents

Illustrations

Pictures Nos. 4, 6, 7, 8, 9, 14, and 18 are from the Mansell Collection; No. 19 is from a private collection; the remainder are from the Radio Times Hulton Picture Library. The authors and publishers are most grateful for permission to reproduce the illustrations.

THE CLEVELAND
STREET AFFAIR

Prologue

It is not surprising that the royal scandal which sprang from the discovery on July 4, 1889, of a male brothel at 19 Cleveland Street in the West End of London has remained for over eighty years the most elusive and mysterious affair of Queen Victoria's reign. There were many heterosexual scandals involving the royal family, and despite heroic attempts to hush them up a large part of the embarrassing truth leaked out to the public. Not so with the homosexual affair of Cleveland Street. For the Victorians this one was almost too hot to handle — only the peripheral "facts" were ever publicized, and these largely thanks to one remarkable radical maverick called Henry Labouchere.

Sex in any form, even that sanctified by that most heavyweight of domestic institutions, Victorian marriage, was acknowledged by the right-minded middle classes with embarrassed reluctance. Very often it generated only fear and anger. Unsanctified or illicit sex, prostitution in particular, was even more bothersome psychologically. Still, try as they might, the upright bourgeoisie were hard pressed to avert their righteous gaze from the estimated 120,000 female prostitutes walking London's streets in the late 1880s — some authorities have suggested that of all women in the central London area, one in eight was involved in prostitution of one kind or another.

The gradations defy analysis, but Henry Mayhew's sociological masterwork, *London Labour and the London Poor*, arrives at no less than six categories during the second and third decades of Victoria's reign: "kept mistresses and prima donnas" standing at the top of a tree which descends via "independents" and "low lodging house women" to "park" and "thieves" women at the bottom of the heap. The exploitation involved is explicit in the terms he used — the numbers escalated towards the geographical center. Hippolyte Taine, the French historian, recorded with evident Gallic satisfaction that there was no way the problem could be disguised or ignored: "Every hundred yards in the Haymarket or the Strand one jostles twenty harlots."

Throughout Victoria's reign, groups like the Society for the Suppression of Vice in London were goading the Commissioner of Police to do the impossible and cleanse the town of what was called The Great Social Evil. Taine, more Rabelaisian but equally disgusted, preferred "the foul hindquarters of English life." There was plenty of ostensibly pious reclamation work. Groups of noble ladies met to pray for their fallen sisters, and W. E. Gladstone, four times Liberal prime minister and the archetypal Victorian paterfamilias, managed to reclaim "a dozen persons" to his "complete satisfaction" after three years of roaming the streets looking for fallen women. His political colleague, Henry Labouchere, did not know that the prime minister often concluded these excursions with solitary sessions of self-flagellation, but was sharp enough to detect the "Grand Old Man's" ambivalent gift for combining "missionary meddling with a keen appreciation of a pretty face. He has never been known to rescue one of our East End whores. . . ." But there were no prayer meetings for homosexual prostitutes or their clients. Here, as Oscar Wilde's lover, Lord Alfred Douglas, said, "was a love that dare not speak its name."

Yet there was scarcely any gap between heterosexual and homosexual forms of prostitution at the grass-roots level. The "gay ladies," as they called themselves, were finding identical areas of the London West End increasingly patrolled by male prostitutes from the middle 1860s onwards. (The men also liked to refer to themselves as "gay," anticipating our contemporary usage; however, they were most often called "poufs," "Mary-Annes," or "Marjeries.") A historian noted that Leicester Square was a refuse heap, and the streets behind it, running across Shaftesbury Avenue and the Charing Cross Road, abounded with "night-houses" crowded with cardsharpers, pickpockets, pugilists, moneylenders, tradesmen known as "shop-boys," and prostitutes of both sexes. The main pubs for "gay" men were the Crown in Charing Cross Road and the Windsor Castle in the Strand.

A guidebook for visitors to the capital, several editions of which appeared in the late 1870s, was called *More Sprees in London — A Guide for Every Green-Horn*. It recommended various brothels (where "gay" women could be found), but also thought it necessary "for the safety of the public" to provide warnings because of "the increase of these monsters in the shapes of men." It favoured harsher penalties, "without which there can be no hope of crushing the bestiality," and went on: "The wretches are too well paid — principally supported by rich companions — to care a jot for a few months imprisonment. Why has the pillory been abolished? Can such monsters be held up to too much public degradation and punishment?

"In the neighbourhood of Charing Cross you will see notices in the windows of many respectable public houses — 'Beware of Sods'. They generally congregate around picture shops . . . when they see what they imagine to be a chance they place their fingers in a peculiar manner beneath the tails of their coats, and wave them about which is their method of giving office."

Writing in 1887, H. S. Ashbee (alias "Pisanus Fraxi"), the foremost authority on pornography and the erotic life of the period, bracketed homosexuality (of which he strongly disapproved) with flagellation, and noted an upsurge in both activities. "This is a fact and did not discretion forbid it, it would be easy to name men of the very highest positions in diplomacy, literature and the army who at the present day indulge in these idiosyncracies, and to point out the haunts they frequent. . . ."

In more conventional publications homosexuality was, literally, unprintable. The scanty and often inaccurate press reports of the Cleveland Street scandal were littered with euphemisms and sentences such as *The Times*'s unctuous "there followed evidence we cannot report." Private and official documents concerning the affair are heavy with a sense of shock and horror. (Female homosexuality, curiously, was not an offense in English law, for when the Criminal Law Amendment Act of 1885 was introduced and shown to Queen Victoria, no one could be found who had the courage to answer her query of "why were women included in the Act

[6]

as surely it was impossible for them?" Her Majesty's notion of a Lesbian was an inhabitant of the Greek island of Lesbos.)

The section of the Criminal Law Amendment Act that dealt generally with "gross indecency" between men was known as the "Labouchere Amendment" after Henry Labouchere, the politician who introduced it. The original intention had been to inflict deterrent sentences, ranging from seven years' hard labor to life imprisonment, upon those convicted. But Parliament, too embarrassed to debate the question fully, or possibly reluctant because there were known homosexuals among its members, reduced the status of the offense to a misdemeanor punishable by a maximum of two years' hard labor. (If the procuring of minors was involved, the maximum penalty was life imprisonment.)

Politicians, reflecting the views of the middle-class electorate, had no desire to go into detail on such a subject. Sometimes it seems as if this same inhibition has afflicted modern historians of the period. The generally excellent semiofficial biography *King Edward VII* by Sir Philip Magnus, published in 1964 (and recently made the basis for a popular British TV series), is meticulously accurate on most aspects of the Prince of Wales's career before and after coming to the throne. Yet Magnus devoted only one paragraph to the Cleveland Street scandal of which the first sentence runs: "The Prince [of Wales] was shocked and amazed again when, in October 1889, the superintendent of his stables, Lord Arthur Somerset, of the Blues, whom he always called 'Podge' and treated as an intimate friend, was discovered in a homosexual brothel which the police raided in Cleveland Street, off Tottenham Court Road. . . ." The sentence, uncharacteristically, contains two errors of fact — the raid was in July, not October, and "Podge" was not discovered in the brothel though he had been a habitué — and gives no hint of the scandal's real implications. It is as if Magnus perceived a Victorian nightmare, shuddered, and moved on as rapidly as possible. For contemporaries the affair opened up unthinkable perspectives, enough to make any respectable Victorian recoil. The Establishment reflex was naturally to cover up.

Our investigation, based primarily on the previously secret records of the Director of Public Prosecutions in the Public Records Office in London which have now become available for the first time, shows that the principal architects of the cover-up were none other than the Prince of Wales himself and Lord Salisbury, the Prime Minister. Both were acutely aware of how damaging a homosexual scandal could be to the integrity of the Throne.

Outwardly, no institution looked more secure than the British monarchy. Queen Victoria, by then in her seventy-first year, had survived the unpopularity of her middle years and the Crown had become inextricably linked with the mythology of Empire. The late 1880s and 1890s represented the high tide of self-conscious imperialism in which British politicians rearranged the world's territories like counters on a Monopoly board. But the careless assumptions of Empire needed the cloak of a sentimental symbol to be acceptable. Queen Victoria, the little old lady always dressed in black, provided it to perfection. The rabidly patriotic English even managed to convince much of the rest of the world to accept them at their own valuation. *The New York Times*, in an editorial comment on the Queen's Diamond Jubilee, could write: "We are a part, and a great part, of the Greater Britain which seems so plainly destined to dominate this planet."

Lytton Strachey, in his famous biography of Queen Victoria, perceived the subtle change in the status of the monarchy most accurately when he wrote:

With the rise of imperialism, there was a change. For imperialism is a faith as well as a business: as it grew, the mysticism in English public life grew with it; and simultaneously a new importance began to attach to the Crown. The need for a symbol — a symbol of England's might, of England's worth, of England's extraordinary and mysterious destiny — became felt more urgently than ever before. The Crown was that symbol, and the Crown rested upon the head of Victoria. Thus it happened that while by the end of the reign the power of the sovereign had appreciably diminished, the prestige of the sovereign had enormously grown.

Symbols of prestige need far better public relations than effective functioning parts within a constitution. And a symbol of this colossal dimension could scarcely be sustained without some human cost to those who were responsible for its maintenance. Victoria's longevity, adding the popular sentiment for age to the sentiment for a bereaved widow, was a gift to the imperial idea. But that same longevity imposed stresses that threatened the human foundation of the whole myth. These were felt most strongly by the Queen's own son, Edward, the Prince of Wales and Heir Apparent, and by his son Prince Albert Victor, the Heir Presumptive. By the time of the Cleveland Street affair in 1889, the strain of the long wait for the job they were born to do was beginning to tell on both of them.

The Prince of Wales was forty-eight years old and showing signs of wear, which was not surprising for a man whose idea of a satisfactory light breakfast ran to grilled oysters served with caviar, and whose personal French chef presided over a staff of sixty. His tailors had had to confess their art unequal to disguising the royal girth; the Prince, long known to his intimates as "Bertie," had acquired an additional nickname — "Tum, Tum."

The Prince's pleasures were by no means restricted to those of the table. He devoted himself with the same zeal to the cult of the wardrobe (uniforms and decorations always fascinated him, and "Prince de Galles" chequered tweed was only one of his personal gifts to the world of male fashion), as well as the turf (his horse won the Derby three times) and the casino (by 1874 his personal debts amounted to a staggering £1.5 million). His sexual tastes were also extravagant and voracious without, it must be said, exhibiting the slightest trace of homosexual leanings.

His life-style had come to assume an almost predictable rhythm. In August he went to Cowes on the Isle of Wight for the yacht races; in September he went abroad, usually to one of the fashionable resorts in Germany; in October he went to Scotland for the deer-stalking; during the winter months he hunted, shot, and made forays to visit friends from his base in Sandringham; in the early spring he went to the French Riviera; and at the beginning of May he came to London for "the Season," which went on for three months and marked the high point of the year for the set that revolved around his official residence in Marlborough House. He rarely missed a race meeting at Goodwood or Ascot, while the Grand National at Aintree and the Derby at Epsom always found him in the royal box. The annual movable feast was invariably garnished with a generous sprinkling of visits to Paris. The Prince liked to dispense with the services of the royal coachman and hired public cabs, and thus he paid his famous calls from *cinq à sept*, hours still reserved for adultery in France in honor of his memory.

So the Prince acquired little honor but plenty of mistresses in both England and France. Sarah Bernhardt, the great tragic actress, liked to imply that one of her children had royal blood. La Goulue, the most celebrated courtesan and cancan performer of the period, immortalized by Toulouse-Lautrec, was on good enough terms with the future King of England to say when he entered the Moulin Rouge in Montmartre: *"'Ullo Wales, est-ce que tu vas payer mon champagne?"* (The Austrian ambassador to London, Count Deym, recording the incident, noted incredulously that the Prince did pay for her champagne, too.) At Cannes in March 1889, the Prince attended the Battle of Flowers as the devil, garbed in scarlet with horns protruding from his head. It was not exactly dignified but, although the Prince's behavior was anathema to his mother, the public at large seemed to have reached a consensus of acceptance, sometimes reluctant and grudging, particularly in church circles, and sometimes envious and tolerant.

The problem posed by Cleveland Street was the gap between tolerance of heterosexual promiscuity, which the Prince of Wales had taken about as far as it could be stretched, and the horror evoked by the specter of homosexual prostitution, which was not supposed to exist at all. The long succession of discarded mistresses may have rendered Bertie himself immune to homosexual rumormongering, but his own son had no such immunity.

Prince Albert Victor Christian Edward, Heir Presumptive, next in line to the Throne after the Prince of Wales, provoked anxiety and bitterness within the royal family almost from the moment of his birth. He was delivered, two months premature, after a royal skating party in January 1864 and his mother, Princess Alexandra, learned of the Queen's decision to call him Albert from a six-year-old child in the royal household.

The Queen then had a notion that all future kings of England should be called Albert after her deceased consort. Alexandra and the Prince of Wales responded to this usurpation of their parental prerogatives by always calling the child "Eddy." In any event, it rapidly became evident that Prince Eddy, like his father, was hopelessly unequal to the task of living up to the legend of the high-minded Prince Consort.

He was partly deaf, withdrawn, and almost incapable of learning. His loud voice, probably a compensation for his hearing defect, annoyed the Queen. She complained that he and his younger brother George, later George V, were badly brought up, implying it was their parents' fault. In 1879, the two princes, Eddy, then thirteen, and George, twelve, were sent on a world tour aboard H.M.S. *Bacchante* and pictures of them tying knots survive. After two years of cadet training had yielded poor results, the examinations had to be made easier so they could pass.

There was a lot of high-flown talk about the merits of life in the Queen's navy but a more realistic appraisal might be found in Sir Winston Churchill's later sour comment on "naval traditions," which he said consisted of nothing more elevated than "rum, buggery and the lash." The persistent rumors of Eddy's homosexuality are attributed by one of his biographers, Michael Harrison, to the naval initiation rites which he believes the princes underwent. "These consisted of two parts: a short, sharp initiation involving the stripping of the initiate, a 'belaying' on the bare buttocks with a leather-dirk scabbard, and as the climax . . . the filling of the luckless cadet's rectum with tallow (later changed to Lifebuoy soap)." Harrison maintains that this tradition survived the naval reforms of 1863.

Queen Victoria would not know of such alarming goings-on but she evidently worried about the boys "purity." In

1880 the Prince of Wales wrote to reassure her about her grandsons' innocence: "We both hope and think that they are so simple and innocent, and that those they have come in contact with have such tact with them, that they are not likely to do them any harm." There are few surviving comments about Prince Eddy from within the royal family that do not contain a note of anxiety. From adolescence onwards he became a magnet for the most sinister rumors. During the *Bacchante* voyage, for instance, a false press report reached England announcing he had been assassinated. Later he was alleged to have secretly gone through a form of marriage with a totally unsuitable "bride," a girl who was both a commoner and a Roman Catholic. Later still, popular myth made Eddy a candidate for the title of Jack the Ripper, whose most spectacular murders were performed in 1888. This rumor seems to have derived from his period at Cambridge and his association with the strange tutor chosen to complete his postnaval education, the legal scholar J. K. Stephen, who later went mad and was one — of many — on the police suspect list for the murders.

"J.K.S.," as he was called, was an enormous man of striking good looks and great physical strength. He created a sensation when cast in the role of Ajax in a university play. His persuasive charm is mentioned by many contemporaries, and after one meeting in 1883, the Prince of Wales, to whom Stephen explained his views about how the young should be educated, was ready to entrust his son's further education to the eventual author of these lines:

> *If all the harm that women have done*
> *Were put in a bundle and rolled into one*
> *Earth would not hold it*
> *The sky could not enfold it*

It could not be lighted nor warmed by the sun.
Such masses of evil
Would puzzle the devil
And keep him in fuel while Time's wheels run . . .

Stephen expressed in virulent form a tradition of misogyny that lingered in the older universities well into the twentieth century (as late as 1930, Julian Bell, a descendant of the Stephen family, described the female students, by then well established in the university, as "bottled snakes").

After his Cambridge period, which ended in 1885 with award of an honorary degree of Doctor of Law, Prince Eddy again assumed a position at the forefront of the royal family's intimate concerns. After some discussion it was decided that he should discontinue his naval career and enter the army instead. As it turned out, the regiment chosen for him — the Tenth Hussars — had privately established an awesome reputation for dissipation and excess.

Prince Eddy was twenty-five years old when the Cleveland Street scandal began to break publicly, and already seemed to be a potential candidate for the title of the strangest English monarch since Edward II. He was a tall, thin young man with long sloping shoulders and a taste for dressing up. A famous portrait of him at the time, showing him posing against a backdrop of studio rocks and trees, amused even contemporaries who were accustomed to the convention. With his sporting tweeds and kilt, he wore a stiff collar of exaggerated high cut and two-inch cuffs appropriate for a state reception. Labouchere, on the strength of it, dubbed Prince Eddy, "Mr Collar and Cuffs." Like so many of his nicknames, it stuck. Such fragile human material for eventual kingship might be able to survive light mockery but it seemed likely to shrivel in the heat of a full-blown scandal.

[14]

❊❦{ ONE }❦❊

"The Abominable Crime
of Buggery"

The story begins on Thursday, July 4, 1889, in the head-quarters of the General Post Office, an imposing red brick building constructed in Victorian Gothic, which dominated St. Martin's-le-Grand in the heart of the City of London. Here a Post Office constable called Luke Hanks was interrogating a fifteen-year-old messenger boy called Charles Swinscow about a series of thefts of small sums of cash. Swinscow was in trouble because he had been reported for carrying what in the circumstances seemed a suspiciously large sum of money — eighteen shillings (a modest fortune in those days; later that year the London dockers went on strike for ten weeks to win an increase of *one penny an hour*, bringing their hourly rate up to sixpence).

The substance of P.C. 718 Luke Hanks's interview with Swinscow is recorded in detail in the policeman's official report, written up in his own businesslike copperplate shortly after the event. Swinscow was, it seems, all injured innocence at first, protesting:

"I did not have so much as that but I had fourteen shillings."

"Where did you get it?" asked Hanks.

"I got it for doing some private work away from the office."

"For whom?"

"For a gentleman named Hammond."

"Where does he live?"

"At nineteen Cleveland Street near Middlesex Hospital."

"What kind of work did you do for him?"

"Will I get into any trouble if I tell you?"

"I cannot say."

"Must I tell you?"

"Certainly."

"I will tell you the truth," said Swinscow. "I got the money from Mr Hammond for going to bed with gentlemen at his house."

Up to this point Hanks's mind was still clearly fixed on the question of petty theft. This was a characteristic obsession of the service — their reputation for absolute probity was just as important to them as the reliability of the mails.

Since Rowland Hill had established the famous "penny post" in 1840, the distinctive blue uniform had become a badge of honesty. It was a necessity; the major banks were yet to establish a wide network of branches, so most small money transactions were handled via the post office, often in the form of postal orders which were in effect checks that could only be cashed at a specified office. No postal employee "whilst engaged in the carriage of Her Majesty's mails" was allowed to carry cash or any other personal belongings, a rule that was rigidly enforced. Even items like tobacco had to be deposited in a locker room, where the staff also changed into uniform before beginning work. Every postal worker had to be "clean," and there were regular spot checks, even when no losses had been reported.

These were conducted by the Post Office's own autonomous police force which if necessary worked in cooperation with the London Metropolitan Police at Scotland Yard — it was not unusual for middle-aged "Bobbies" who were tired of pounding the beat and saw no promotion prospects to transfer to the postal police, where the hours were easier. The skill with which Hanks elicited a damning statement from Swinscow suggests long experience — Hanks was, as will be seen, an unusually conscientious man. He decided that Swinscow's startling admission was sufficiently important for him to suspend the interrogation and report at once to his superior officer, John Phillips. Armed with Phillips's instructions to take as full a statement from the boy as possible, he returned straightaway. Swinscow, without benefit of legal advice, then committed himself in the following terms:

I was fifteen years of age on the 14th September last. I am now a Boy Messenger in the General Post Office. . . . I made the acquaintance of a boy named Newlove who was then a Boy Messenger in the Secretary's office and is now a 3rd Class clerk. . . . Soon after I got to know him he asked me to go into the lavatory at the basement of the Post Office building — we went into one water closet and shut the door and we behaved indecently together — we did this on other occasions afterwards. In about a weeks time Newlove said as near as I can recollect "Will you come to a house where you'll go to bed with gentlemen, you'll get four shillings each time?" I said at first "it wouldn't do" but he persuaded me at last and I went with him to 19 Cleveland Street near Tottenham Court Road, near the Middlesex Hospital. He rang the bell and the door was opened by a boy about my own size.

[17]

We went into a parlour on the ground floor and saw a gentleman there who I have learned since is the proprietor. His name is Hammond. He said — good evening I'm very glad you've come. I waited a little while and another gentleman came in. Mr Hammond introduced me, saying that this was the gentleman I was to go with that evening. I went into the back parlour i.e. a room on the same floor with the gentleman. There was a bed there. We both undressed and being quite naked got into the bed. He put his penis between my legs and an emission took place. I was with him about ½ an hour and then we got up. He gave me a sovereign which I gave to Mr Hammond who gave me four shillings. I have never seen this gentleman again. I went once more to the same house and only once. It was about a month ago.

The Swinscow statement introduced an entirely new slant to the investigation — from now on the question of theft is absent from the records of what took place (although we can be fairly sure that some other Post Office policeman found himself going through the cumbrous processes leading to the discovery and arrest of the forgotten petty thief). Luke Hanks, who had begun his investigation with the aim of eradicating one form of small dishonesty, had stumbled on what seemed to the Post Office a much more gross kind of corruption. Already they knew that two of their uniformed employees were involved (since Henry Newlove, the class-three clerk, had now been implicated by his friend Swinscow). Now they had to find out whether the corruption went further. And the fact that Newlove worked in the particularly sensitive telegraph branch was an added impetus to the investigation.

For St. Martin's-le-Grand was no ordinary post office. It handled domestic mails as a matter of course. But the Central Telegraph Branch's responsibilities were infinitely wider. St. Martin's-le-Grand now looks distinctly shabby and run-down; in a word, "Victorian." But to Hanks and his fellow employees it must have seemed the very epitome of humming modernity. Eight years later, when the Queen celebrated her Diamond Jubilee, one bizarre scheme for underlining the importance of the occasion was that each one of her by then three hundred and seventy-two million subjects should send her a congratulatory telegram. As James Morris notes in *Pax Britannica*, this bright idea "was fortunately not pursued"; instead, *she* sent *them* a telegram via St. Martin's-le-Grand. Seen from this perspective, it is easy to understand why "the Service," as the postal functionaries referred to their enormous department of state, had become sacrosanct.

In modern terms the equivalent to the reaction of Hanks and his superiors at finding the nucleus of a homosexual network operating in their own headquarters would be the discovery that some vitally important government department had been made "insecure" after being infiltrated by aliens. It was as if they had found spies in their own citadel. And this (to modern eyes disproportionate) response to a fairly mundane situation explains the passion that went into the investigation. Swinscow, the unfortunate fifteen-year-old who was worried about "getting into trouble," had no idea of the forces he had let loose as a result of his adolescent peccadilloes.

The statement was still not full enough for Hanks: he wanted more names, and got them. Swinscow now mentioned two more postal employees, a boy called Wright and another whose name was Thickbroom (a subject of mirth, no doubt, at 19 Cleveland Street). Swinscow told Hanks that Newlove had also persuaded these two to visit Hammond's house. They were sent for immediately and confirmed what Swinscow had said, thus implicating Newlove a second time in his role of procurer. There was no time to waste. By the end of Thursday afternoon, a matter of hours after Swinscow's first hesitant and fearful admission, all three boys and Newlove himself had been suspended from the service. They were no longer considered worthy to wear its uniform.

On Friday morning Hanks again reported to his superior John Phillips, who in turn sent a report yet higher up to the office of the Postmaster-General himself, the Right Honorable Henry Cecil Raiker. At this point the case was regarded as sufficiently important to bring in the Metropolitan Police and its head, Commissioner James Monro. He assigned his best detective, Inspector Frederick G. Abberline, to take charge of the case. Since Abberline was at this period in charge of one of the most famous criminal investigations in history, the search for Jack the Ripper, whose attacks on prostitutes had brought terror to the East End of London, it is clear that the Cleveland Street affair, even at this embryo stage, was already receiving priority treatment.

This impression is confirmed by Abberline's own haste, to which the sacred Victorian middle-class weekend was at once sacrificed without compunction. The inspector arranged for a special sitting of the Marlborough Street magistrates' court to be convened for Saturday morning. The three boys (but not Newlove) appeared before it, no doubt still wondering what had hit them. By noon Abberline had what he wanted in his hands — warrants for the arrest of Charles Hammond and Henry Newlove, framing the charge in language of such threatening *gravitas* that the boys must have trembled to hear it: "that they did unlawfully, wickedly and corruptly conspire, combine and confederate and agree to incite and procure George Alma Wright and divers other persons to commit the abominable crime of buggery."

But Charles Hammond remained one step ahead of the law. A man in his early forties, he was long accustomed to the hazards of living on the edge of society and charting his erratic path to avoid the pitfalls laid for him by such as Inspector Abberline. Newlove had managed to get him a warning; and, whatever flaws there may have been in the Cleveland Street proprietor's moral fiber, when it came to the instinct for self-preservation no elements were lacking. To him the message was loud and clear: only months earlier a clergyman convicted of charges less grave than those he anticipated were about to be laid against himself had been sentenced to penal servitude for life. Hammond paused only to warn Newlove that he must "stoutly deny everything" — a piece of reassurance that was to ring very hollow in the days to come. Having thus discharged his responsibilities to his youthful confederate, Hammond was free to concentrate on the subject most exercising his mind, his own freedom and security. He packed his emergency kit in a black portmanteau, and took off at once for the port of Gravesend, twenty miles downriver from London, where his brother lived.

Abberline soon found he was up against a fugitive of talent and experience. While Hammond's associates at St. Martin's-le-Grand were left to face the police, he himself was busy arranging his passage on the first available packet boat to France. The impressive resources of Scotland Yard were now marshaled against him, and Inspector Abberline, heading a squad of experienced men, dramatically descended on 19 Cleveland Street. All to no avail. For the fussy, overdecorated premises, crammed with the antimacassars and pianos, the caged linnets and dyed ostrich feathers, which for Hammond were prerequisites of a genteel Victorian domestic scene, had by now taken on the lonely air of the *Marie-Celeste* after her crew had vanished. There was every sign of the late proprietor, including his dirty laundry. The man himself had vanished, leaving Abberline and his posse fuming with frustration.

The dogged P.C. Hanks must have shared this frustration, but he pressed on with his own relentless investigation, which by now was keeping him busy virtually round the clock. Sunday, July 7, was no day of rest for him. The pious Victorian Sabbath, when respectable people abjured work as punctiliously as they avoided any activity that might be construed as amusing, now had to be foregone in the interests of a more pressing set of moral imperatives. Hanks sought out Newlove and arrested him at his home in Bayham Street, Camden.

When the warrant for his arrest had been read out to him, Newlove remarked that after he had been suspended from duty he had confided in another member of the post office staff called Hewett, who, he claimed, had introduced him to Hammond in the first place. Hewett had persuaded him to warn Hammond. Newlove seemed aggrieved that Hewett had not been charged as well. Hewett, like Hammond, had made himself scarce. Newlove was so upset by Hewett's escape that he forgot Hammond's warning to deny everything and began to sing an even more interesting song than the unfortunate Swinscow. The first verse was to Constable Hanks as they walked to the police station, which Hanks laconically noted down in his report. "On the 7th of July I was taking Newlove to the Police Station when he said to me 'I think it very hard that I should get into trouble while men in high position are allowed to walk about free.' I said 'What do you mean?' and he replied 'Why, Lord Arthur Somerset goes regularly to the house at Cleveland Street, so does the Earl of Euston and Colonel Jervois.' " Constable Hanks did not hand this statement to Inspector Abberline at the time, as it was his duty to hand it in first to his own superiors at the Post Office. It is likely he mentioned it to Abberline, but even if he did not, Newlove saved him the time by volunteering the same information to the inspector the following day. This time he added that Lord Arthur was known in the house as "Mr. Brown," and that he "had to do with me on several occasions." The principle of naming names had been established.

The name of Lord Arthur Somerset immediately elevated the status of the whole inquiry. Then thirty-eight years old, Lord Arthur had been an intimate of the royal family since infancy. On the surface he seemed an impeccably hearty and virile member of the royal entourage — a cavalry officer who like his father, the eighth Duke of Beaufort, kept an eye on His Royal Highness's bloodstock. His official title was Superintendent of the Stables and Extra Equerry. The Beaufort family (motto: "I scorn to change or fear") owned the great Palladian-style mansion of Badminton in Gloucestershire and a handy 52,000 acres of surrounding countryside over which they hunted with great relish. Even before the Cleveland Street affair became public, the family had a well-publicized track record of sexual aberration. Lord Arthur's father was notorious for his liking for "unripe fruit" as prepubescent girls were called, and subsidized a procuress called Madame Marie in Conduit Street in order to ensure a regular supply. His wife was a byword among contemporaries for her capacity to "rise above" her husband's extramarital activities, very much like Alexandra with the Prince of Wales. On one occasion a butler unwrapped by mistake an oil painting of the Duke's latest infant mistress in front of thirty luncheon guests. "His Grace would probably like it in his private apartments" was her only comment, delivered without a blink. Lord Arthur's elder brother, Henry, was less conveniently wed. He had married and had a child by a French

[23]

heiress named Isabel. After eighteen months of marriage Isabel made "certain disclosures" about her husband's conduct with a footman that convinced her mother, who was staying at Badminton, that her daughter should not spend another night under that roof. Lord Henry's wife and mother-in-law left, never to return again.

Hanks was now free to delve deeper into the lives and family relationships of the postal employees. By the following Tuesday, July 9, these inquiries took him to the lower-middle-class north London area of Camden Town, and to the home of Newlove's mother at 38 Bayham Place, Bayham Street. Ostensibly, he was visiting Mrs. Newlove at the request of another member of her family, Newlove's brother. In fact, he was sniffing around in the hope that some further illuminating detail might be forthcoming.

While Hanks was interviewing Henry Newlove's mother there was a knock on the door. "Why," said Mrs. Newlove, "that's Mr. Veck's knock." Hanks remembered the name — a telegraphist named Veck had been dismissed from the Gravesend staff some years earlier for homosexual offenses with messenger boys. Since then he had been calling himself "The Reverend" George Veck (among other names). Hanks moved discreetly into the passage while Mrs. Newlove let in her new caller, and overheard their conversation.

Veck was saying that he had visited Hammond at Gravesend the previous day but, calling there again that same morning, he had discovered Hammond had now gone abroad. The caller promised expansively to look after her unfortunate son's interests. "If you want any money just let me know. I will instruct a solicitor to defend Henry in the morning."

Hanks reported this conversation as soon as he returned to the Post Office; in due course it reached Inspector Abberline. He was not noted for his scrupulous attention to the book — already on the Jack the Ripper case he had mistakenly arrested two innocent men and held them on suspicion. Among his further suspects were, extraordinary though it seems, two distinguished figures with royal links, one of them the royal physician, Sir William Gull, and the second J. K. Stephen, Prince Eddy's Cambridge tutor.

Abberline had considered the possibility that the Ripper's identity was to be found on the fringes of the royal household. Newlove's statement, naming "Podge" Somerset, may have made him suspect that this case might also clear up the identity of the Ripper. If so, he was to be disappointed.

His superior was Commissioner Monro, who was relatively new to the job. He had previously been head of the detective branch and was well liked by the men in the force. He was unusual for a senior policeman of that time as he was blessed with a social conscience. Monro must have realized that the Cleveland Street affair was developing into a case that presented an embarrassing and difficult conflict between his conscience and his relationship with his superiors.

Abberline asked for permission to put 19 Cleveland Street under permanent surveillance, and Monro agreed. If positive identification could be obtained of some of the customers of the house who might not know Hammond had fled, then convincing his superiors would be much easier. P.C. Sladden, of Tottenham Court Road police station, was put on watch.

Sladden's reports survive. Dozens of men called at the house, many being well dressed, while others are described as soldiers, a bombardier, a corporal in the Life Guards. Sladden followed one or two of the more prosperous-looking. One turned out to be a Member of Parliament, another a member of the National Liberal Club. On July 10 the watch began to reap major dividends:

July 10. 2:05 P.M. Hammonds sister in law entered with an-other woman.

4:50 P.M. A man query-[*sic*]Lord Arthur Somerset rode up in a hansom cab, rang bell and was answered through the door. He then looked at his watch and waited till 5:10 P.M. when a Corporal of the 2nd Battal-lion Life Guards met him, apparently by appointment. They shook hands and talked together for five minutes and then went off towards Oxford St.

July 11. Veck entered 1:26 P.M.

July 12. 8:25 A.M. Van belonging to Saunders Bros of 7 Southampton Street removed Goods.

10:05 A.M. Veck left.

July 13. 4:15 P.M. Lord Arthur Somerset and Corporal same as before.

Sladden's reports convinced Abberline that Newlove's claim was the truth, and this belief was strengthened when Veck produced the solicitor for Newlove. He turned out to be an egregious character named Arthur Newton, aged twenty-eight, who practiced law from offices almost next door to Marl-borough Street police court. Newton tended to act for clients who had embarrassing cases and in this case Abberline was sure that neither Veck, Hammond, nor Newlove had the means to pay Newton's fees for his rather specialized services. He reasoned that it had to be Lord Arthur who would be picking up the bill.

By July 19, Monro and Abberline felt they had a solid case

[26]

against Lord Arthur as well as Newlove and the absent Hammond. In serious cases it was the convention for the police to hand over the files to the Treasury Solicitor who then conducted the case on behalf of the state. Commissioner Monro submitted the complete dossier to Treasury Solicitor Sir Augustus Stephenson, together with a request that extradition proceedings be commenced to bring Hammond back from France. Here the police case received its first setback.

Sir Augustus wrote to Monro explaining that he recalled from a similar scandal some years previously that a decision had been taken at the "highest level" that in cases of this character it was "public policy not to give unnecessary publicity." Sir Augustus returned the poisoned chalice by suggesting that the police should handle the prosecution of the case themselves through their own solicitor: "If," Sir Augustus observed, "you feel in some difficulty, then you should consult the Home Secretary." Monro went straight to the Home Secretary, Henry Matthews, who decided that the case should be handled by Sir Augustus. His decision was undoubtedly influenced by the fact that Monro was able to tell him that two of the post office boys, Swinscow and Thickbroom, had been taken by Constable Sladden to the cavalry barracks in Knightsbridge and positively identified Lord Arthur as one of their customers. Matthews also endorsed Monro's request for the extradition warrant for Hammond.

The Public Prosecutor's department accepted Matthews's decision with ill-concealed reluctance. It was obvious to all concerned that if there were any errors in the presentation of the case, and the eventual trial resulted in Lord Arthur's acquittal, then the careers of all concerned could come to a sudden halt. Their fears cannot have been allayed by the first manifestation of the Prime Minister's interest in the case.

[27]

The third Marquess of Salisbury, whom Queen Victoria regarded as the ablest of the prime ministers who came and went during her long reign, was the epitome of all the patrician virtues and defects. He was head of a family which had served Country and Crown since his ancestor Lord Cecil had been the confidant and spy-master of Queen Elizabeth in the sixteenth century. He was an intellectual, interested in science and religion, but subject to bouts of depression and what sometimes seemed like an omnidirectional malice. Benjamin Disraeli, who respected Salisbury's abilities and was no slouch himself at invective, once described the Marquess as "a master of jibes, and flouts and sneers."

In the era of "Splendid Isolation" for Britain, few individuals seemed more splendidly isolated than its Prime Minister. He made little secret of the fact that he preferred the privacy of his laboratory in Hatfield, the Cecil family seat, or the remoteness of his house in France, to the collective tedium of Cabinet meetings. "British policy," he once said, "is to drift lazily downstream, occasionally putting out a boathook to avoid a collision." Few men had a greater understanding of the imperial mythology and its value in preserving the dream of power while Britain drifted away from its reality. He himself was free from the flamboyant visions of imperialism but took good care to see that all the important threads of power came into his hands. Since 1886 he had doubled in the office of Foreign Secretary as well as Prime Minister. The routine matter of authorizing an application for Charles Hammond's extradition from France came to the Foreign Office in mid-July 1889. It would not normally be considered a matter that needed to exercise the considerable brain of the nation's leader. The Home Secretary, Henry Matthews, who made the application on behalf of Scotland Yard, can scarcely have expected that Lord Salisbury would show any personal interest in so mundane a topic. On Wednesday, July 24, Home Secretary Matthews received the following communication from a Foreign Office official:

Sir
    The Marquess of Salisbury has given his careful consideration to your letter of the 22nd . . . relative to the case of Charles Hammond charged with conspiring to incite certain persons to commit unnatural offences, who is believed to have escaped to Paris.
    I am now directed to inform you . . . that his Lordship does not consider this to be a case in which any official application could justifiably be made to the French Government for assistance. . . .

Matthews got the hint that too diligent an inquiry into the Cleveland Street affair might not be in everyone's best interests, although it was some time before the hint became broad enough to impress all the public officials concerned in the case.

    The London "Season" in 1889 was in no way disrupted by the ominous portents in the Cleveland Street case. No mention of it had appeared in the press and the aristocracy could enjoy all the splendor and ostentation of a brilliant season. There were the normal parades, operas, drives in the park, luncheon parties, and magnificent balls. The ladies, as usual, made a point of changing their clothes three or four times a day. The gentlemen were impeccable in riding clothes, frock coat, or tails. The visit of the Shah of Persia, who stayed in England throughout the entire month of July, added an extra touch of Eastern mystery to the frivolities. The Shah was extremely polite, and memories of one of his predecessors who had caused the Queen some distress by sacrificing a sheep on one of the best carpets in Buckingham Palace were happily erased. The Prince of Wales, who was obliged to bear most of the expense of the Shah's entertainment, kept smiling bravely. Several friends, among them Lord Cadogan, Lord Rosebery, the Rothschilds, and Sir Albert Sassoon, rallied round by providing extra festivities.

Prince Eddy, with his moustache impressively curled up at both ends, had made something of a public impact and was in constant attendance on the Shah. In London's East End a woman called Alice McKenzie was murdered on the night of July 16/17 and reckoned to be another victim of Jack the Ripper. The murder occurred at a time when Prince Eddy could not possibly have been in the vicinity of Whitechapel. Thus tongues wagging about the possibility of Prince Eddy being the Ripper were stilled.

All in all, it had been an expensive and exhausting but not altogether unsuccessful season for the royal family. Cleveland Street, if they were aware of it at all, was a cloud considerably smaller than a man's hand.

TWO

A Close Friend
of Mr. Brown

The first consequence of turning the case over to the Treasury Solicitor was a further delay. The second was — or ought to have been — a higher degree of professionalism in its preparation. By the late 1880s the Treasury Solicitor's department under Sir Augustus Stephenson had become a highly effective part of the government's legal apparatus with a strongly ingrained sense of public service.

This was a comparatively recent development, though the office of Solicitor to the Treasury dated back to the year 1655 and Oliver Cromwell's period as Lord Protector. In the seventeenth and eighteenth centuries the Treasury Solicitor was something of a legal odd-job man, a solicitor in private practice who had the government as one of his many clients. Early in the nineteenth century the task was upgraded. In 1806 the post was assigned to a barrister who was required to give up his private practice and devote himself exclusively to Treasury work. Yet he was still somewhat remote from the center of affairs, and most of the early-nineteenth-century Solicitors to the Treasury worked out of offices in Lincoln's Inn, over a mile away from the main offices of state in Whitehall. But with the rapid expansion of government business came the need for a more flexible and accessible legal service. By the middle of the century the Treasury Solicitor found himself acting for a wide variety of other government departments besides the Treasury itself, among them the Foreign, Colonial, and Home Offices. In 1851 the department was finally established in the Treasury building.

By 1880 it had added the War Office and Admiralty to its range of bureaucratic clients and been given charge of bankruptcy prosecutions. The opinion of the Treasury Solicitor's office was almost invariably taken before criminal prosecutions were initiated by any government department. In 1884, under the terms of the Prosecution of Offenders Act, the Treasury Solicitor formally became the Director of Public Prosecutions with powers defined by statute. The DPP was obliged to carry out prosecutions in cases involving the death penalty and in those where "the importance or difficulty of or other circumstances" required his action "in the public interest." He also had to conduct prosecutions when ordered by the Home Secretary or the Attorney General. It was in his role as the DPP that Sir Augustus Stephenson formally took charge of the Cleveland Street case.

He was not, however, an entirely free agent in the conduct of a case. Under Section 10 of the regulations defining his duties as DPP was the requirement that he should be subject to the "direction" of the Attorney General in all matters, including the selection and instruction of counsel. In normal circumstances this requirement was scarcely more than a formality, but in the Cleveland Street case it was to provide an unending source of friction. Unlike Sir Augustus Stephenson, Sir Richard Webster, the Attorney General, was not a very decisive man.

Sir Richard was an amiable if somewhat sanctimonious man, valued by his Tory colleagues as a solid performer in the House of Commons but, in his public utterances at least, inclined to be boring. (The Parliamentary sketchwriter of *Reynolds's Newspaper* once reported: "Uriah Heep, the Attorney-General, made one of his tedious, laboured replies for which he is famous. Sir Richard Webster really ought to have been a female evangelist, instead of a lawyer.") The son of a judge, Sir Richard grew up with an appetite for the heartier Victorian activities. At Oxford he won the mile and two-mile races. He delighted in playing billiards and singing drawing-room songs in a booming tenor voice. He was called to the bar in 1868 and took silk (became a Queen's Counsel) ten years later. His earnings at the bar were prodigious and, like many successful nineteenth-century lawyers, he decided to go into politics in middle life. He entered the Commons in 1889 first as the Tory member for Launceston in Cornwall and subsequently sat for the Isle of Wight. Lord Salisbury promptly gave him ministerial office as Attorney General.

Contemporaries were somewhat puzzled by Sir Richard's spectacular earning power as a counsel, as he was neither learned nor particularly clever. Nevertheless, he had an exceptional talent for putting his clients at ease. Generous and genial by nature, he was a regular churchgoer and it was said that he did not have a malicious bone in his body. The Cleveland Street affair was to put this easygoing personality under almost intolerable stress.

Some of the stresses were built into the system. As a party

politician, and the Tory government's chief spokesman on legal issues in the House of Commons, he was naturally subject to pressures that were no concern of the Treasury Solicitor's department. He also, unlike the legal eagles in the Treasury, still maintained a thriving private practice. In 1888 and 1889, for example, he acted as leading counsel for *The Times* newspaper before the Parnell Commission — set up to determine whether Charles Stewart Parnell, the charismatic leader of the Irish Nationalists in the Commons, had a hand in the Phoenix Park murders (the allegation that he had, printed in *The Times*, was found to be based on forgeries penned by one Richard Pigott, who later committed suicide). Although there is no evidence in the records of the Cleveland Street affair to indicate that Sir Richard's indecision was prompted by a specific conflict between his public and private sources of income, the case's capacity for alienating the aristocracy — and with it some of the wealthiest potential clients for his services at the bar — cannot have added to his appetite for the proceedings. In 1895 the government decided that the Attorney General must henceforth abandon his private practice during his period of office. It was a long overdue reform.

In the initial stages of the inquiry Sir Richard's involvement was as marginal as it had been in most of the previous cases handled by the Public Prosecutor. The main task as the DPP's department saw it was to test the strength of the police's case against Newlove, Hammond, and Veck, as well as Lord Arthur Somerset. They were in almost daily communication with Scotland Yard's Inspector Abberline but preferred to accept nothing on trust. Although Labouchere and other opponents of the Government subsequently charged the DPP's department with complicity in a cover-up, the private files of the department, which have recently become available for public inspection, do not support this charge — at least in the early stages. The DPP was given the case on July 25 and completed the time-consuming but necessary process of reinterviewing all the post office boys and taking depositions by August 1. On August 3, the DPP solicited a preliminary opinion from Horace E. Avory, one of the counsel who had been asked to conduct the prosecution in court. Avory was cautious but not negative. He felt that the Foreign Office was wrong in ruling out the possibility of having Hammond extradicted and recommended further efforts on this front. He did not want to proceed until all efforts to give Hammond his day in court had been exhausted. The opinion does not mention Lord Arthur Somerset by name but concludes with what is presumably a reference to him by saying: "I do not think the evidence at present justifies any proceedings against the person said to have been identified by the two boys." Scotland Yard, however, took the sensible precaution of stationing a man outside the Knightsbridge barracks to keep an eye on Lord Arthur's movements in case he might take it into his head to leave in a hurry. On August 7, the policeman recorded Lord Arthur's dignified presence in the review, on the occasion of a State Visit by Kaiser Wilhelm, the German emperor. It was a magnificent event, marred only by the absence of the Prince of Wales who excused himself because an attack of phlebitis made it difficult for him to mount his horse. If Somerset was worried by the abrupt closure of the establishment in Cleveland Street, he certainly gave no hint in his public appearance to betray the fact.

By the end of the first week in August Sir Augustus Stephenson had completed his review of the police case against Newlove and Hammond, and forwarded his assessment of the evidence against Veck and Lord Arthur Somerset to the Attorney General. On Saturday, August 10, Sir Richard Webster came back with an ostensibly firm opinion, cosigned by Mr. Avory and the Solicitor General, Sir Edward Clarke. It read as follows:

We are of opinion that proceedings should be taken against the man Veck alias Barber and also against Lord Arthur Somerset. There is not at present any sufficient evidence against the other parties except Hammond to justify proceedings. As regards Veck he should in our judgment be arrested on warrant founded on a sworn information on the charge on which Newlove is now remanded. As regards Lord Arthur Somerset summons should in the first case be issued against him to appear to answer a charge under Section XI of the Criminal Law Amendment Act 1885. The question whether any further charge should be preferred against Veck or Lord Arthur Somerset must depend on the course of proceedings.

Section XI (the Labouchere Amendment) of the Criminal Law Amendment Act, 1885, under which Lord Arthur Somerset was said to be liable, reads: "Any male person who, in public or private, commits, or is a party to the commission of, or procures or attempts to procure the commission by any male person, shall be guilty of a misdemeanor, and being convicted thereof shall be liable at the discretion of the court to be imprisoned for any term not exceeding two years, with or without hard labour." Thus, in just a little over two weeks the police case against Lord Arthur Somerset had been effectively transformed into a Public Prosecutor's case with full authority to proceed. By nineteenth-century standards this was in no way evidence of dilatoriness; it was, on the contrary, exceptionally fast work.

Much too fast, as it turned out, for the liking of Lord Salisbury. On that same Saturday, Home Secretary Matthews fired off three letters. Two in his own hand went to Sir Augustus Stephenson. The first asked the DPP to proceed no further on the case until they had had an opportunity to confer. The second instructed him to obtain the necessary breathing space by asking the magistrate for a remand in Newlove's case, on the ground that "there is an expectation of bringing Hammond, the principal offender, before the court." Matthews's third letter, dictated to an official, was sent to Sir Richard Webster, the Attorney General: "Mr. Matthews wishes you to stay your hand until he has seen Lord Salisbury on Monday morning. Mr. Matthews will let you have his final decision before 2 P.M. on Monday. It would be well I think for you to be at the Treasury from 12–1 on Monday in case you should be sent for to see Lord Salisbury."

No record survives in the documents which became available of what Lord Salisbury's instruction or "guidance" was on that Monday. But it was remarkable that the Prime Minister, who had no legal training, should have intervened in a prosecution involving a misdemeanor and on which all the relevant law officers were in broad agreement. Equally remarkable was Matthews's instruction to the DPP. The Home Office fully accepted Lord Salisbury's earlier ruling that no request for Hammond's extradition could be made, yet at the same time the Secretary of State was instructing the DPP that Newlove should be remanded — for the third time — because there was an expectation of Hammond's being brought before the court. Mr. Matthews could have had no such expectation. Moreover, there was not, under the statute, any reason why the Home Secretary should give orders to anybody on the case. He could instruct the Treasury Solicitor to take a case but final responsibility for its conduct lay with the Attorney General alone.

By this stage, however, lines of authority were becoming

increasingly vague. Despite the Foreign Office's ruling against Hammond's extradition, both the Post Office and Scotland Yard had men in France keeping watch on his movement. Inspector Abberline, just back from Paris, reported "confidentially" to the DPP that the sin-hardened Parisian police were not likely to put themselves to much trouble on the case unless strong diplomatic pressure was brought to bear. The overall situation on the Cleveland Street case by the end of the second week in August did not yet perhaps amount to a cover-up but one of near total confusion with several public authorities pulling in radically different directions.

Sir Augustus Stephenson's tidy mind was affronted by the disorder. On August 17, he wrote a piteous memorandum to Matthews at the Home Office, pointing out that Section 10 of the regulations circumscribed his role as DPP, and submitted that "I am a statutable officer . . . and that it is not only expedient but necessary that I should receive the direction of the Attorney-General." He was also concerned about the responsibility imposed on him by Section 8 of the same regulations which, broadly, obliged the DPP to carry on prosecutions that had not been proceeded with in "reasonable time" by other authorities. The implication was that Sir Augustus felt that his department — for want of proper instructions — was being put in the position of imposing unreasonable delays on the action. Justice delayed, then as now, was justice denied.

On the question of "direction" Sir Augustus did not have long to wait. He received it later that same day. Sir Richard Webster, after further sessions with the Home Secretary and consultation with Lord Halsbury, the Lord Chancellor, now saw the evidence in a somewhat different light. He wrote to the DPP: "I have read the further statements of Thick-broom, Swinscow and PC Sladden which have been taken since the Solicitor-General Mr. Avory and I advised in this case on the 10th. inst. These statements differ on important points from those previously before us and I am not satisfied with the evidence of identification of Lord Arthur Somerset. I therefore give you directions that no proceedings shall be taken against him until further directions have been given. I direct the proceedings against the man Veck be taken in accordance with the opinion of the 10th August." It was not the view of the DPP's department that there were any significant discrepancies between the supplementary statements, other than on points of detail, but any "direction" was better than none.

On August 19, the police applied to the Marlborough Street court and obtained a warrant for Veck's arrest. At seven o'clock the next morning they burst into Veck's lodgings in Howland Street off the Tottenham Court Road and found a seventeen-year-old boy in his bed but no "Reverend" Daniel Veck. The boy said his name was George Barber and described himself as Veck's "private secretary." He explained that his employer had gone to Portsmouth but was expected back by train later that day. The police met and arrested Veck at the railway station and found some very intriguing documents in his possession. They were particularly interested in those relating to a "Mr. Brown" and somebody called Algernon Allies, then living at 16 Gregory Street in Sudbury, a sleepy town in Suffolk, some fifty miles northeast of London. On August 23, the relentless post office policeman, Luke Hanks, was given the chance to visit Sudbury and find out who Allies was and what he had to say.

He found a good-looking, curly-haired boy of nineteen living at home with respectable working-class parents. His father was a coachman in service. The story of Algernon Edward Allies fascinated P.C. Hanks. Allies also knew Lord Arthur Somerset as "Mr. Brown," but on a much more intimate basis, it seemed, than either Thickbroom or Newlove. He had met Lord Arthur while working as a page boy in the Marlborough Club. Unfortunately, he had lost his position there in October 1887 after being arrested and found guilty of stealing sixteen pounds, eight shillings from a member of the club. He had spent one day in prison for that offense. After Allies's release, Lord Arthur had come to his aid and taken him for a short time to live with him at his private address in 19 Hill Street. Subsequently Lord Arthur had given him a letter of introduction that had secured him lodgings with a Mr. Hammond in 19 Cleveland Street. He and Lord Arthur met there regularly and went to bed together. Hammond had admitted him "as a friend of Mr. Brown." He had heard something about the recent troubles of Mr. Hammond and the difficulties in Cleveland Street but did not know the details. He had left some months before the post office boys were rumbled. Lord Arthur Somerset had supported him for some time — he usually got about fifteen shillings a week — and written him many endearing letters signed "Brown." He did not have the letters. He had received an anonymous letter on the day before P.C. Hanks's arrival, requesting him to destroy all letters from "Mr. Brown." He did not know who had written that letter but he had burned Lord Arthur's correspondence as requested. He did, however, still have in his possession three postal orders for twenty shillings each, as yet uncashed, which had been enclosed in the last letter from Lord Arthur. They were dated 20 August (by not very amazing coincidence the day of Veck's arrest) and had been despatched from a post office in Knightsbridge near Lord Arthur Somerset's barracks. In his final letter to him, said Allies, Lord Arthur had indicated that he might be going away for some time. The young man told P.C. Hanks that he was prepared to come to London with him and make a clean breast of it all to the appropriate authorities. P.C. Hanks told him to start packing his things.

Once back in the city, the complaisant Allies was trundled straight round to the office of the Treasury Solicitor to make a full statement. He agreed to put himself under the protection of Inspector Abberline and was found lodgings over the Rose Coffee House in Hounsditch, a genteel but dismal establishment on the frontier between the City and London's East End. The police, now certain of their case against Lord Arthur Somerset, wanted to keep a very close eye on their prize material witness. The wisdom of this policy was proved on the day after Allies's departure for London when his parents' humble home in Sudbury received another unexpected caller. This time it was a gentleman called Augustus De Gallo, who worked as an interpreter at Marlborough Street police court and as a part-time inquiry agent for the solicitor Arthur Newton. De Gallo seemed upset to find Allies had already gone and asked if he had left any letters behind. Mr. Allies said he had not.

Sir Augustus Stephenson, apparently as impressed as the police by the importance of Allies's story, immediately forwarded the fresh evidence to the Home Secretary. It is not clear why Sir Augustus should have first referred the Allies material to the Home Secretary rather than the Attorney General but it seems probable that the DPP had shrewdly decided that Sir Richard Webster was not going to amount to much more than a rubber stamp for decisions made by his political superiors. In any event, Matthews replied severely a day later:

I have read the additional papers in Reg v Newlove. The principle accepted by the Attorney-General was that a charge of this sort ought not to be preferred unless the evidence was complete, and gave moral certainty to a conviction. The additional papers contain only the evidence of a participant in the offence, which would not be sufficient in law to warrant a conviction unless it was corroborated by untainted evidence. The evidence in question stands peculiarly in need of corroboration; the story of numerous letters, all destroyed, seems very suspicious. So far as I am able to judge, it appears to me that there is not sufficient evidence to justify proceedings against LAS at present. PS. This is a case in which I think any "directions" should be given by the AG [Attorney General] himself.

It is difficult to fathom why the Home Secretary should have been so inflexible, unless he, too, was the subject of pressures of which the DPP's department had no knowledge. (At that point Sir Augustus Stephenson seems to have been unaware of Lord Salisbury's interest in the case.) Henry Matthews, then sixty-three years old and a bachelor, was a considerable man and anything but a conventional Tory hack. Although the Home Secretary was not required to have any special facility in legal matters, Matthews had a lifetime of experience in the law. He was born in Ceylon, the son of a judge, and brought up, in accordance with his mother's faith, as a Roman Catholic. On the family's return to England, his father's wealth and service to the cause of the empire ensured his son's position in society, but the young man still suffered from the legally sanctioned discrimination against Catholics. Oxford and Cambridge were barred to him. In consequence, he was educated in Paris and at London University before being called to the bar. He was a brilliant and witty advocate and in 1868 achieved the double distinction of taking silk and being elected Member of Parliament for the Irish constituency of Dungarvan. He won the seat by the princely margin of 157 votes to 105 and in later life Matthews attributed this famous victory to his skill in having combined the nationalist and Tory votes against his Liberal opponent "at the cost of 800 bottles of whisky." But no amount of alcohol could long preserve his hold on the constituency in an era of increasingly strident Irish nationalism. In the election of 1874 Dungarvan rejected him and it was another twelve years before he was reelected to the House of Commons, as the member for East Birmingham. But he had kept up his political acquaintance, particularly with Lord Randolph Churchill — a close personal friend— and he returned in style. Salisbury immediately appointed him Home Secretary over the heads of many who had done much longer service on the back benches. He thus became the first Catholic to achieve Cabinet office since the passing of the Emancipation Act of 1829. As minister, he was more popular with his department than he was in the Commons. The opposition likened him to a "French dancing master" and some of his more reactionary Tory colleagues inclined to the view that he was a shade too clever for their liking. Home Secretaries, however, were rarely popular figures in the nineteenth century (nor are they, for that matter, in the twentieth). Their authority over much of the apparatus of state control — most notably in the areas of police and citizenship — inevitably saddled them with the more disagreeable kind of publicity. And in an age when capital punishment was the automatic penalty for murder, the Home Secretary, as the final reviewing authority (on behalf of the Crown) in controversial cases, held down the most thankless of judicial responsibilities. Matthews's personality failed to triumph over the unpleasant nature of his work, but he was, nonetheless, a respected figure. Few doubted that he did his duty, however disagreeable it might be, as he saw it.

This reputation made his obdurate refusal to reassess the Cleveland Street case all the more baffling to the staff in the DPP's office. Matthews might not relish the grisly publicity that would inevitably accompany a charge of "gross indecency" against an aristocrat and member of the royal household, but he did not appear to be the kind of man who would deliberately put obstacles in the way of prosecution if the facts led in that direction.

If it came down to a matter of concern for the image of the royal household, Sir Augustus Stephenson had more reason to be personally concerned about this than Matthews or any other member of the Cabinet. His own brother, of whom he was very fond, was, like Lord Arthur Somerset, an equerry of the Prince of Wales. But the facts of Lord Arthur's case led, in Sir Augustus's view, overwhelmingly in one direction. On August 27 he set them out in a long memorandum for the consumption of Secretary Matthews and Sir Richard Webster. The matter was pressing as the committal hearing to decide whether Hammond (in absentia), Newlove, and Veck should stand trial was about to start before Mr. James Lennox Hannay, the magistrate at Marlborough Street police court. The press normally attended these hearings, and if Lord Arthur Somerset's name was mentioned either by the post office boys or Allies, there was little chance of a public scandal being avoided. The evidence against Somerset, in the DPP's opinion, consisted of the identification evidence of Thickbroom, Swinscow, and P.C. Sladden; the fact that Newlove had volunteered the name of Somerset, alias "Mr. Brown," to the police before their identifications took place; and the corroboration testimony of Algernon Allies. Putting these elements together, Sir Augustus wrote: "Whoever 'Mr Brown' or 'LAS' may be, it is I submit — on the statements already taken, that there is *some* man who has been known or has given one or the other of these names who has been in the habit of frequenting No. 19 Cleveland Street and there committing statutable misdemeanors and under circumstances (in my judgement) under which a jury might come to the conclusion that felonies also had been committed." Sir Augustus mentioned that this imposed a threefold responsibility on the authorities: first, it was the duty of the police to try to identify the "LAS" mentioned in the statements; second, it was the duty of the prosecution in the case against Newlove and the others to submit their evidence fully to the magistrate "without regard to what the consequences may be to this individual — be he 'Mr Brown,' 'LAS' or any other man"; and third, they had a duty to the police to ensure that "their evidence should not be discredited by withholding any evidence (*i.e.*, on 'LAS') which would tend to confirm their statements." In a supplementary memorandum, written two days later, Sir Augustus dealt with the "possibility" that the original evidence against "Mr. Brown/LAS" might have been the result of a conspiracy by the post office boys Thickbroom, Swinscow, and Newlove. He conceded that such a conspiracy might have been conceivable, but argued that it did not explain how Allies, who had left Cleveland Street and gone home to live in Suffolk well before the police moved in on the case, should independently come up with the same version of the "Mr. Brown/LAS" story. Conspiracy theories, in short, really would not wash.

The response of Attorney General Sir Richard Webster was delayed for a while. He had gone up to Scotland to get away from it all for a few days. But Secretary Matthews was still at his post and becoming increasingly irritated. His temper was not improved by the quality of the carbon copies of the DPP's memoranda — "flimsies" as they were known in Whitehall. On August 29, Matthews wrote furiously to the DPP: "I have strained my eyes, not overgood at this moment, over your 'flimsy', and I must enter a protest against being asked to read documents so illegible. . . ." Nor did Secretary Matthews feel much rewarded by what he had managed to decipher — "I find nothing to suggest any fresh charge." The DPP should, as previously instructed, concentrate on the cases against Newlove and Veck.

On the following day, Sir Augustus had his resolve strengthened by more evidence of support from his own staff. The Honorable Hamilton J. Cuffe, the able assistant DPP, had returned from holiday and completed his reading of the papers in the case; he was completely in accord with the director's view of it. On August 31, a Saturday, Sir Augustus decided to further strain the Home Secretary's eyesight and produced yet another memorandum, eight pages in length and more highly moralistic in tone. (At weekends, perhaps as a result of the propinquity of the Sabbath, Sir Augustus's ethical views become even more sharply pronounced than usual.) He told the Home Secretary: "[T]he *moral* evidence against LAS is overwhelming. I am fully conscious of the public scandal — and the advisability of avoiding it — which this charge against LAS might create — and deeply sympathise with his family — I have no sympathy whatever for him personally. That is for the Mr Brown or LAS (who I believe to be an existing person) who is described by the boys Thickbroom and Swinscow — and by the boy Allies as taking him from the Marlborough Club to 19 Cleveland Street and keeping him as he might a woman in his pay — who has been seen *though it is not evidence* . . . in company with a private soldier. I am quite aware that although it is a legal offence to keep a bawdy house — it is not a legal offence to keep or frequent a house kept for the accommodation of sodomites — but it is in my judgement also a public scandal . . . if no steps can be taken to deprive such persons of HH Commission and to enforce their retirement from Society. . . ."

As far as the legal aspect of the case was concerned, Sir Augustus's view was that "The evidence against LAS *may* be insufficient to justify a charge being preferred against him but — such as it is — in my judgement and with very great respect I say it is *stronger* than that against Veck against whom a charge has been preferred. I may state that this is also the opinion of Mr Avory [the counsel instructed by the DPP]." It was perhaps as close as so staid a public servant could come to expressing an opinion that responsibility for a double standard, sanctioning one law for the rich and another for the poor, should rest on the conscience of his superiors. But the DPP's conclusion was submissive enough: he assured Secretary Matthews that the case would be conducted in strict accordance with his instructions. Lord Arthur Somerset was still, officially, in the clear.

The Prince of Wales was still blissfully unaware of any suggestion of scandal touching his old friend "Podge" Somerset. After the departure of Kaiser Wilhelm, the Prince had set off for Homburg in Hesse, Germany, for what he hoped would be the start of a three-month vacation. But the resort proved less congenial than in former years and, after complaining in a letter to his younger son George of the importunity of "uninteresting and tiresome people," he abruptly returned home. By the end of August he was at his ease in Scotland, staying with his daughter and son-in-law at Mar Lodge.

THREE

Playing the Slap-Bum Polka

The men from Scotland Yard continued their dogged investigation. It centered on the Soho area. On August 10, Inspector Abberline came up with a quite sensational potential witness — "John Saul, of 150 Old Compton Street, of no occupation," as he was described in the sworn statement the police extracted from him on that day.

Saul was obviously anxious to appease the police with whom he had established some kind of accommodation in which they left him free to develop his interests in the Haymarket and Strand unharassed while he in return gave information — on this occasion mainly about Charles Hammond, the one-time "Madame" of Cleveland Street, who had been the first to scent the danger and leave. It is apparent from Saul's statement that Hammond was no stranger to the midnight flit, the last train out of town before trouble started.

"I know Charles Hammond who lately lived at 19 Cleveland Street, Fitzroy Square. The photograph produced is a good likeness of him. I have known him since the 1st May, 1879." Thus began Saul's account of Hammond's career, which at certain points had overlapped his own — they had something in common. "We both earned our livelihood as Sodomites."

The word itself comes out of the old pages with a whiff of actuality. Here for a moment is the dismal "gay" world on the fringes of Soho which had become Saul's natural habitat. Not that he hadn't aimed higher, but his best days were over. He was by then in his late thirties and reduced to peddling his aging charms to a lower class of person; he felt a bit sorry for himself and a bit spiteful.

Hammond's own career had also had its ups and downs. "I used to give him all the money I earned often times as much as £8 and £9 a week. I lived with him till the early part of December 1879." They had parted, come together, and parted yet again several times in the following years. Hammond kept on the move, changing addresses, usually in the Soho area. He also married "a French prostitute named Madame Caroline with whom he has always lived." They had arrived in Cleveland Street in 1887, and Saul had stayed "for about 5 weeks. I then had a row with him and have not spoken to him since."

This was a strange remark, for if it were true, what kind of information could he possess about the previous six months in which the police were mainly interested? Still, Saul was able to describe Hammond's recent business with eyewitness precision and even revealed the source of what might be called the "post-office connection." Saul stated: "A gentleman named Captain Le Barber used to visit the house and bring boys down with him. He used to get the boys situations in the Post Office service." The house was visited by some very

[49]

grand names; Saul had always been a snob and recorded gradations of rank a bit pedantically.

"Major ———— a brother of the firm of wine merchants — used to visit the house as a Sodomite. Hammond wears a gold seal on his watch chain which the major gave him. I identify the seal on his photograph." Others named included a colonel, a gentleman living in Richmond Terrace, Whitehall, and a tailor in Jermyn Street; a banker at the corner of the Haymarket, described as "a short gentleman with a fair moustache," was a constant visitor at the house.

Having delivered these small-fry, Saul produced, with a certain pride, his big fish: "The young Duke of Grafton, I mean the brother of the present Duke, was a constant visitor at Hammond's. He is a tall, fine-looking man with a fair moustache." In the margin of the statement there is a scribbled note by a later author, whose initials are now illegible, to the effect that "the Earl of Euston," which is in fact the correct title of the next-in-line to the Grafton dukedom, "has been mentioned by Newlove."

This disclosure was enough — for the time being anyway — to satisfy Inspector Abberline. Saul obviously left the station with a promise to be back with more. Two days later, on 12 August, there was another statement from him, duly signed and witnessed. It is clear that he is trying to make the very best of his material, which provided only meager additions to his earlier statement. Saul was obviously desperate to please Abberline. He brought along three visiting cards of professional "Mary-Annes" (which have survived in the records, a bit thumb-stained) and he started telling tales about two of their owners under their pseudonyms "Clifton" and "Canning."

"They used to go frequently to Hammond's with the young Duke of Grafton, I mean, as I said before, the present

Duke's brother. . . . He went to Hammond's with me on one occasion. . . . He is not an actual Sodomite. He likes to play with you and then 'spend' on your belly. 'Canning' is called 'Lively Poll'. . . ."

Abberline put the statements safely away, thinking no doubt that they might come in handy later as evidence. But although they assumed considerable importance some weeks later through being shown to a third party, they were never actually produced in a courtroom. They survive, however, and in tandem with another eccentric document of the period — the two gold-bound volumes of *The Sins of the Cities of the Plain* (clandestinely published as a limited subscription edition in 1882) which contain John Saul's slightly touched-up "Recollections of a Mary-Anne" — they provide some earthy insights into the underground aspect of Victorian life which until recently has been little known. As Virginia Cowles observed in her study *Edward VII and his Circle*, "the Victorian creed of duty and respectability . . . made little headway with the two extremes of society — 'the swells' and 'the roughs'." However, using the two sets of source material, it would be easy to construct a tale with a moral of the kind that middle-class Victorians themselves would have approved, although they would have objected to the subject matter. For the story would be of the decline of a "Mary-Anne," ravaged by time and the evil nature of his calling — it was a widespread Victorian belief that female prostitutes invariably died within a few years of joining the profession, though, inconveniently for the myth, "Skittles" Walters, companion of the Prince of Wales and Labouchere and so many others, the acknowledged queen of her calling, died after World War I in her mid-eighties. But Saul fitted the stereotype even to the extent of ending his statement with a justification which might have come straight from the mouth of an abused housemaid. "I am still a professional 'Mary-Anne'. I have lost my character and cannot get on otherwise. I occasionally do odd jobs for gay people" — a last, pathetic attempt to suggest that he and the Victorian work ethic were not entirely at odds. It seems unlikely that Inspector Abberline was much impressed.

Only eight years before it had been a very different story, when Saul was first observed by "Mr. Cambon," the editor of Saul's own memoirs, who had spotted the likely lad in Leicester Square.

He was dressed in tight-fitting clothes, which set off his Adonis-like figure to the best advantage, especially about what snobs call the fork of his trousers, where evidently he was endowed by nature by a very extraordinary development of male appendage; he had small and elegant feet, set off by pretty patent leather boots, a fresh-looking beardless face, with almost feminine features, auburn hair, and sparkling blue eyes which told me that the handsome youth (ah, youth no longer) must indeed be one of the Mary-Annes of London. . . .

Just so. The author's eyes did not deceive him and his passion for note-taking provides us with an account of a classic Victorian pick-up and a well-drawn sketch of the "Mary-Anne" as a young man. The author confessed nervousness about behaving too outrageously in a public place and made his approach with discretion. He suggested a glass of wine in a public house, but the young man turned out to be as cautious as the author himself. He was more taken with the prospect of "somewhere quiet."

"Would you mind if we take a cab to my chambers — I live in Cornwall Mansions close to Baker Street Station —

have a cigar and chat with me. I see you are evidently a fast young chap and can put me up to a thing or two."

"All right. Put your thing up, I suppose you mean. Why do you seem so afraid to say what you mean?"

They set off by hansom cab and the author gradually overcame his reticence, aided by a meal which consisted of "rumpsteak with oyster sauce and two bottles of champagne of an extra sec brand." Once the table had been exhausted the author mixed "a couple of good warm glasses of brandy hot," and said: "My boy, I hoped you enjoyed your dinner but you have not favoured me with your name." His own, he said, was "Mr. Cambon."

"Saul, Jack Saul, Sir, of Lisle Street Leicester Square, and ready for a lark with a free gentleman at any time. What was it made you take a fancy to me? Did you observe any particularly interesting points about your humble servant?" and he shyly looked down. . . .

"You seem a fine figure and so evidently well hung that I had quite a fancy to satisfy my curiosity about it. Is it real or made up for show?"

"As real as my face sir and a great deal prettier. Did you ever see such a fine tosser in your life?"

The inquisitive "Mr. Cambon" wasted no time in verifying this assertion of Saul's virility and noted:

He had a priapus nearly ten inches long, very thick, and underhung by a most glorious pair of balls which were surrounded and set off by quite a profusion of light auburn curls. I hate to see balls hang loosely down, or even a fine prick with small or scarcely any stones to it — these half and half tools are an abomination. . . . "By Jove," I exclaimed.

"It's my only fortune, sir," Saul replied. "But it really provides for all I want."

And so they proceeded to make love in front of the coal fire, "Cambon" thereby establishing that Saul's skills extended to birching and a gift for fellatio described in ecstatic terms appropriate to a contemporary *Deep Throat*.

After resting awhile, and taking a little more stimulant, I asked him how he had come to acquire such a decided taste for gamahuching to do it so deliciously as he did.

"That would be too long a tale to go into now," he replied. "Some other day, if you make it worth my while, I will give you my whole history."

"Could you write it out, or give me an outline so that I might put it into the shape of a tale?"

"Certainly, but it would take me so much time that you would have to make me a present of at leasty twenty pounds. It would take me three or four weeks several hours a day."

"I don't mind a fiver a week if you give me a fair lot, say thirty or forty pages of note-paper a week, tolerably well written," I replied.

And Cambon also suggested the "Recollections of a Mary-Anne" title, which at first Saul disapproved of, insisting that "low girls of the neighborhood called him that when they wanted to insult him." However, on more mature consideration the young man decided to overcome his sensitivity on this score — "the four fivers will make up for that."

A week later he returned with the first section of the manuscript impressively headed "Jack Saul's Recollections. The Early Development of the Pederastic Idea in his Youthful Mind."

Saul begins on a courteous yet businesslike note: "Dear Sir — I need scarcely tell you that little cocks, and everything relating to them, had a peculiar interest to me from the very earliest time. . . . I was born of well-to-do people of the farmer class in Suffolk. . . ." And so the various stages in Saul's career are recorded. His early sexual experiences encompass the familiar territory of milkmaids (and naturally stable boys) before he is sent to Colchester to attend a school which bears some resemblance to Dickens's Dotheboy's Hall. (We learn that it was subsequently closed after a local scandal. This is not altogether surprising since according to Saul's description its specialities would have put a Tangier bordello to shame. On the first night his fellow inmates draw lots for the new arrival as the prelude to a gang-bang involving "a kind of chain" of eight pupils sodomizing each other. This first night, as Saul recounts at great length, is more or less typical, although as he admits, "it was sometimes necessary to go in for a general suck all round and give our bottoms a rest.")

With such an education behind him there is little doubt about the young man's future métier. It was assured when "soon after reaching the age of 16 my mother succeeded in getting me placed at Messrs Cygnet and Ego's, a large West End linen drapery house, which had a most aristocratic connection." And so too, after a certain amount of trouble with his superior, one Mr. Gooser, had Saul. He was instructed to deliver a set of silk fabric samples to the luxurious Mayfair mansion of "The Hon Lady Diana Furbelow," the sister of "The Marquis of Churton." The Marquis, hidden by the traditional screen, surprised young Jack raping his sister, who pretended to have aroused the young haberdasher inadvertently when seized by an attack of cramp in the calf for which she required urgent massage. It was evidently a set-up. Saul had the sister and the brother had Saul, a relationship which with various combinations continued until the hero was dismissed by the conscientious Mr. Gooser and the Marquis was forced to take his nymphomaniac and incestuous sibling abroad for a period of recuperation. Saul was not, however, left empty-handed. The nobleman tipped him twenty pounds and provided an introduction to an establishment off Portland Place where members paid a subscription of one hundred guineas and the proprietor was named "Mr. Inslip."

It is a very thinly disguised description of the Hundred Guineas Club — by far the most extravagant homosexual club of the period, a much grander affair than Cleveland Street, which in comparison emerges as a *maison de passe* — a mere place for "short time" sexual encounters with a few trimmings. At the Hundred Guineas members and their guests customarily assumed feminine names. According to Michael Harrison, in a recent biography of Prince Albert Victor, the Prince was "a regular and popular guest." His assumed name, says Harrison, was "Victoria."

In his memoir Saul presented himself at Portland Place and Mr. Inslip accepted him on the spot — like "Mr. Cambon" some years later, he too was evidently impressed by the "sparkling blue eyes, Adonis-like form" and so forth. The young Saul was turned over for the afternoon to a former cavalry trooper, one Fred Jones, who under Inslip's instructions took him back to his chambers where Saul was treated "to chops and cigars." Jones did not seduce him, however — both of them, he said, must reserve their strength for the night's entertainment. Instead he adopted a fraternal attitude, the sophisticated elder brother explaining the ways of the capital to a kid up from the country. Jones was already an established "Mary-Anne" thoroughly familiar with the homosexual underworld of London. He explained that he started out as a heterosexual but had switched because of the money — and also because homosexuality, like pugilism, was one of the few areas where a poor boy could make his way in the world. In the process Jones had rather lost his taste for the opposite sex, and, as he confided to the eager Saul over the inevitable Havana cigar: "You can easily imagine it is not so agreeable to spend half an hour with a housemaid when one has been caressed all night by a nobleman." Saul was entranced and plied Jones with questions. His answers provided an excellent and detailed picture of the homosexual establishments of the epoch. A series of clubs had been set up, Jones explained, in part because of the recent decease of a certain old lady called Mrs. Truman who had exploited a tobacconist's shop conveniently located next to the cavalry barracks in Albany Street, close to Regent's Park. Her system had been simplicity itself. "The old lady would receive orders from gentlemen and then let us know at the barracks. . . ." According to Jones all army recruits were initiated into sodomy by their N.C.O.'s immediately upon enlistment. "It is surprising how naturally they take to it." Jones himself, originally an amateur like his fellow soldiers, had been bought out by a "gentleman friend" and had set himself up professionally. He reckoned that Saul had done well to settle on Mr. Inslip's since it was the most select (and also best paying) brothel in the West End. The members, many of whom were known only by girls' names, could be trusted implicitly. Saul would see.

After this briefing they returned to Portland Place, where Mr. Inslip was waiting for them. Saul was led into a dressing room, where "I assumed a very charming female costume and so did Fred." Their *toilette* complete, Mr. Inslip delivered his final instructions.

"For the evening, Fred, your name is Isabel and yours, Mr. Saul, is to be Evelyn." They then presented themselves in a long red-plush room adorned with French furniture and occupied by a group of languid dandies drinking champagne as well as some other members "in exquisite female attire." There was dancing, hand-holding, the exchange of small talk, and ambiguous propositions until "at 2 A.M. suddenly all the lights went out and we were in total darkness," a system, as Jones had explained, designed to prevent any of the members from being disappointed. The rule was that the "Mary-Annes" had sex with their chosen partner and were then available for anyone — Saul had been warned "on no account" to reject *any* approach, and indeed there was no way he could have done so since the darkness prevented him from seeing who approached him. "Before time was called about 6 A.M. I had had six different gentlemen, besides one of those dressed as a girl." He returned home with Jones and was given five pounds for the night. Thereafter he became an Inslip "regular," much in demand as he boasted in his recollections to "Mr. Cambon." He had managed to preserve his looks and health by appearing on no more than two evenings a week; otherwise "I would have exhausted my capital."

Saul, subsequently, recorded an evening in Grosvenor Square with an Earl, three page-boys (one black) and "three gentlemen whom the Earl assured us could be found in the pages of Debrett but preferred to be known by their sobriquets — Messrs Wire-In, Cold-Cream and Come-Again." The "Slap-Bum Polka was played."

Saul, alias "Evelyn," was by then well launched into his thesis that almost everyone in high society had homosexual tastes and was constantly occupied in finding ways of satisfying them. As he said, "The extent to which pederasty is carried on in London between gentlemen and young fellows is little dreamed of by the outside public." By the time "Recollections" was written, Saul was in his late twenties and had already acquired a wide range of experience which gives his digressions an authoritative ring.

He was, for example, well acquainted with Ernest Boulton and Frederick Park, two notorious transvestites who featured in a spectacular trial in 1871 and were later immortalized in the limerick:

> *There was an old person of Sark*
> *Who buggered a pig in the dark;*
> *The swine in surprise*
> *Murmured: "God blast your eyes,*
> *Do you take me for Boulton or Park?"*

Saul described a ball given at Haxell's Hotel in the Strand in the company of Boulton and Park. "No doubt," wrote Saul, "the proprietor was quite innocent of any idea of what our fun really was; but there were two or three dressing-rooms into which one could retire at leisure. Boulton was superbly got up as a beautiful young lady, and I observed Lord Arthur was very spooney upon her. He called her Laura. I noticed them slip away together. . . ."

One of the dressing rooms contained a hole in the wall, an indispensable element in Victorian pornography, and through this convenient aperture the young Saul was able to watch "the transports of delight" which followed as the two lovers embraced.

The "Lord Arthur" in question was not Lord Arthur Somerset of Cleveland Street fame but Lord Arthur Clinton, third son of the fifth Duke of Newcastle, who committed suicide before Boulton and Park came to trial. Saul became a close friend of the two transvestites, and after the ball was over was invited to return with them to their chambers where the servants were under the impression they were two fashionable "gay" ladies.

As soon as we got to Boulton's place, he gave me a drop of his invigorating cordial, a lovely liquer which seemed to warm my blood to the tips of my fingers: then we went to bed, slept until about 12 o'clock, and had breakfast all dressed as ladies. Boulton assured me they hadn't a rag of male clothing on the premises, all their manly attire being at some other place. He rose from the breakfast table and opening the piano ran his hand over the keys; then motioning me to accompany him gave me a luscious kiss. "You darling Evelyn. . . ."

Boulton was a young man of many parts, contriving to sodomize Saul while seated at the piano singing "Don't You Remember Sweet Alice, Ben Bolt" to his own accompaniment.

In the second volume Saul relates with mock coyness the story of his attendance at a garden party given in honor of the Prince of Wales on the grounds of "a noble mansion" on the banks of the Thames. His alleged escort was Lord Arthur Clinton.

"I was dressed as a midshipman and I was presented to HRH as the Hon. Mr Somebody, I can't exactly remember the name now. After promenading for some time, we met an elderly gentleman to whom he introduced me. 'Evelyn' whispered Lord Arthur, 'this is Lord H——— who has heard of your attractions; let me introduce and leave you to him.' Lord H——— expressed the greatest pleasure he had in making my acquaintance, adding to Lord A 'that he hoped his young friend was not too shy or mock-modest.'"

Saul was not. "At last we came to a very retired arbour with a seat behind some rockwork and a small fountain playing in front. 'Just the spot for us,' said his lordship. 'Let me sit down here and make a better acquaintance, my dear!'"

Thus "Evelyn," as Saul usually referred to himself, made another conquest — an extremely rapid one, for half an hour later they were back with the official party.

"When we rejoined the company, one of the retinue of HRH begged me for an introduction, and after some little conversation assured me my fortune would be made if I would only consent to visit Berlin and Vienna, as he could introduce me to many of the highest personages in Germany." But Saul, a creature of his jingoistic time, responded: "Not caring to leave Good Old England, I politely declined his overtures, assuring him at the same time that I had not the least objection to being introduced to any of his eminent countrymen, should they happen to visit London."

Saul regarded himself "as a very gentlemanly 'Mary-Anne' " — evidently "Evelyn" was the kind of young lady you could take anywhere. In his memoirs he was very disapproving of other professional male prostitutes who were less scrupulous, for example

young Wilson, a very handsome youth of 16 or thereabouts. He is about 5 feet two or 3 inches; very fair and pretty; with chestnut hair, dark blue eyes and a set of pearly teeth which, combined with the rosy colour of his cheeks makes him an almost irresistable bait to old gentlemen — or for that matter, young ones too — who are addicted to the pederastic vice. We are much in each other's confidence and he has let me into the secrets of his way of doing business. He commenced one afternoon as we were smoking cigars and drinking champagne together at Inslip's.

"Do you think Jack I ever let those old fellows have me? No fear, I know a game worth two of that. You see, I never bring them home with me, and in fact always affect the innocent — don't know where to go; am living with my father and mother at Greenwich or some out of the way part of London, and only came to the West End to look about at the shops and see the swells. If a gentleman is very pressing I never consent to anything unless he asks me to accompany him to his house or chambers. Once got home with him I say: 'Now sir what present are you going to make me?'

" 'Stop a bit my boy 'til we see how you please me,' or something very like that is the answer I generally get.

" 'No: I'll have it now or I'll raise the house, you old sod. Do you think I'm a greenhorn? I want a fiver. Don't I know too well that little boys only get five or ten shillings after it's all over? But that won't do for me so shell out at once or there'll be a pretty good scandal.' "

There is a similarity in this anecdote to another in Saul's statement to Abberline, where he describes the technique of "Mr. Clifton." One of his more profitable lines, according to Saul, was to take gentlemen to his room "where by arrangement two or three men are secreted under his bed, and just as they are performing the men suddenly come out and bounce money out of them by threats."

Saul brings us close to the other side of the image Victorians liked to present to the outsiders and, as far as possible, to themselves. It is a world of sex, violence, blackmail, and, it must be said, considerable humor, some distance from the emotional climate of the proper Victorians, who thought it necessary to call female legs "unmentionables" and who equipped piano legs with fringed shawls in case the nude mahogany provoked lustful thoughts. Still, it was hard to repress the old Adam even in the most "respectable" surroundings. The late nineteenth century was the great era of the double entendre, the smoking room story, and the dirty limerick.

Herbert Ashbee, whose ambition was to catalogue and own every obscene work ever published (he finally bequeathed 15,900 "curious" volumes to the British Museum, including of course *Cities of the Plain*), noted the sexual minutiae of

Victorian life with the dedication of a scholar. Officially sex was nowhere; yet to the repressed Victorians it often seemed to be everywhere even, as Ashbee noted in a characteristic footnote, "in so well-ordered a paper as *The Times*, where I daily discover sufficient errors to fill several pages." One or two of the recent (Ashbee was writing in the late 1880s) "trippings in type" are strange enough to warrant their being recorded. In Number 4, January 23, 1882, page 7, column 4, the following line, "The Speaker then said he felt inclined for a bit of fucking," was inserted by a malicious printer in the speech of a Member of Parliament. In a later issue of *The Times*, the eagle-eyed Ashbee found interpolated in the advertisement for a book entitled *Everyday Life in our Public Schools* the information: "with a Glossary of some words used by Henry Irving in his disquisition upon Fucking, which is in Common Use in those Schools." It was not only *The Times* which found itself bedeviled by malicious printers. *The Morning Post*, an even more Tory organ of the Establishment, had trouble when announcing in its Court Circular the birth of a royal child after a confinement at Buckingham Palace. As Ashbee noted, "The substitution of an 'f' where there should have been a 'b' in the name of the Palace where the confinement took place leant this heading a suspiciously suggestive appearance."

The world that got its charge from sniggering over oblique puns buried in columns of grey printed matter was decidedly not the world of Jack Saul. In retrospect, it is easy to see why Inspector Abberline did not immediately pass Saul's statements on to the Director of Public Prosecutions as evidence for a charge against the Earl of Euston. There is no reason to believe that Abberline was any less anxious to nail Lord Euston than Lord Arthur Somerset (both of whom figured in Newlove's early statement to P.C. Hanks). But the idea of introducing Saul as a witness against anybody — without very substantial corroboration — must have been considered far too risky. He was a real enough person, but to the average middle-class jury he would convey the kind of reality that they did not want to believe could possibly exist.

·»·❧ FOUR ❧«·

Enter the Prince

By the end of August 1889 the fuse on the Cleveland Street affair had burned dangerously low. Although no hint either of the crime or the bitter interdepartmental battle it was causing had appeared in any newspaper, the nerves of participants in the secret drama were beginning to fray. The hierarchy of the Post Office was irritated with the Metropolitan Police for failing to wrap up a case that involved debauchment of their junior employees, wearing, in some cases, the Queen's uniform. (All the boys involved were still under suspension, with pay of twelve shillings a week.) Scotland Yard was chagrined by the ostensible dilatoriness of the Director of Public Prosecutions. The DPP was bemused by the Home Secretary's apparent reluctance to face the facts of the case against Lord Arthur Somerset. The Attorney General, whose responsibility it was to clarify these matters, was in an agony of indecision. Meanwhile Lord Arthur Somerset, whose intelligence system always seemed one step ahead of the authorities, quietly obtained four months' leave of absence from his regiment and took off for the continent.

The news was greeted with something akin to relief in the DPP's department. On September 2, Sir Augustus Stephenson passed on the information about Somerset's departure for foreign parts, without a servant (a fact that he deemed significant), to Sir Richard Webster in the Attorney General's office. "This *may*," he wrote, "be the best thing which could happen." Even so, he was anxious that no imputation could be leveled against the authorities that suggested complicity in Somerset's escaping the eye of public justice. The immediate matter to be decided was how the prosecution should, in its examination-in-chief of the post office boys before the magistrate, handle possible references to Lord Arthur Somerset. Sir Augustus, who had earlier been on the opinion that references to "LAS" should be made without regard to the consequences, was now prepared to compromise.

After much shuffling of paper on this delicate issue the DPP, the Attorney General, and the Home Secretary arrived at what they considered an appropriate solution. Prosecuting counsel was instructed to examine the boys as fully as possible about the description of their clients and even extract their pseudonyms — in Lord Arthur's case "Mr. Brown" — but, on Sir Richard Webster's express instructions, "witnesses . . . should not be asked in chief the names of individuals." It was a strategy that appeared to salve their consciences, but only, as it turned out, by imposing a frightful burden on that of the magistrate, Mr. Hanny. On Wednesday, September 4, after the third day of the committal hearing involving Veck and Newlove, a worried Mr. Hanny buttonholed Sir Augustus Stephenson and voiced his qualms. Sir Augustus mentioned the meeting in a memorandum to the Attorney General on the following day: "After case was over yesterday Mr Hanny the magistrate came to speak with me privately — said that in an ordinary case *i.e.* one that did not concern the Treasury, he would have felt it his duty to call for disclosure of the names and then had it brought before him, by warrant and included in the charge. . . . [H]e wished the Attorney-General to bear in mind his position." Sir Augustus goes on to explain that quite apart from Lord Arthur Somerset there were two other men who had been described in evidence and "whose identity might, without difficulty be established" — one was a Mr. E. G. Ripley, spoken of by George Barber, Veck's "private secretary," as the man who introduced him to 19 Cleveland Street; the other was a "Capt." Montague Barber, whom Newlove had mentioned. The clear implication of the memorandum was that Sir Augustus felt that justice might seem to be proceeding but was not in fact being done.

Nevertheless, the strategy was maintained. Veck and Newlove were committed for trial on September 11 and no mention of Somerset (or, for that matter, Ripley or Captain Barber) appeared in the evidence. The name "Mr. Brown" had been mentioned by Allies, but there was little to distinguish him from London's monstrous regiment of "Mr. Browns." His appearance was variously described by the boys but the general outline was clear:

A very tall man with little side whiskers, a moustache short cut and hair of a light colour.

A very tall man with light brown hair, and side whiskers of reddish hue. He wore his hat on one side.

The man was in evening dress, had red whiskers, rather long, a moustache, a bald head, and was about 6ft 2in or 3in.

A rather tall man with side whiskers, a bald head, and rather fair.

The Times law court reporter devoted one paragraph to the magistrate's hearing, stating that Veck and Newlove had been charged "with conspiring together to induce boys to go into a house in Cleveland Street" and noting that the magistrate refused bail. But William Thomas Stead's lively *Pall Mall Gazette*'s high-class gossip column reported:

We are glad to see that Sir Augustus Stephenson, Solicitor to the Treasury, was present at the Marlborough Street police court yesterday, when two prisoners were committed for their trial in connection with a criminal charge of a disagreeable nature. . . . [T]he question Sir Augustus Stephenson will have to answer is whether the two noble Lords and other notable persons in society who were accused by the witnesses of having been principals in the crime for which the man Veck was committed to trial are to be allowed to escape scot free. There has been much too much of this kind of thing in the past. The wretched agents are run in and sent to penal servitude: the lords and gentlemen who employ them swagger at large and are even welcomed as valuable allies of the Administration of the day.

It was the first hint in public print that Cleveland Street had any potential as a *cause célèbre*. The interest of W. T. Stead made the hint doubly ominous. The son of a Northumbrian Congregational minister, Stead had won his journalistic spurs as a campaigning editor of *The Northern Echo* before coming to London where he found an infinitely better class of muck to rake. He revolutionized *The Pall Mall Gazette*, once described by William Makepeace Thackeray as a newspaper "written by gentlemen for gentlemen." Under Stead's guidance it became decidedly less gentlemanly.

His legendary series in the *Gazette*, "Maiden Tribute of Modern Babylon," furthered the passing of the Criminal Law Amendment Act of 1885, raising the age of consent to sixteen. He also supplied Labouchere with a private dossier on homosexuality that led to the Labouchere Amendment — Section XI — of that same Act which now menaced Lord Arthur Somerset. Stead had paid a price for his notoriety as a campaigner, serving three months in Holloway jail for abducting a girl to give verisimilitude to his "Maiden" series, but he had not lost his appetite for the cause of abolishing sin.

A few days after the appearance of the *Gazette* paragraph, the magazine *Man of the World* pulled the sly, journalistic trick of juxtaposing two *seemingly* unrelated gossip items that "insiders" would know would have been integrated but for the risk of libel. The first item read simply: "Lord Arthur Somerset has left England. He intends to remain abroad for an indefinite period." The second, somewhat more extended, began: "A gross scandal, the like of which has not been heard in England for many years, has been discovered by the police. . . ." The magazine, much read by gentlemen, rounded off the smear with a pious hope that if the case came to court "stringent measures" would be taken to prevent "disgusting revelations" appearing in the newspapers.

Sir Richard Webster, meanwhile, emboldened by the fact that Lord Arthur Somerset had left the country, was preparing for another U-turn in attitude. He had experienced the full blast of Sir Augustus Stephenson's sense of outrage and felt that some kind of punitive gesture should be made, if only to prevent Lord Arthur showing his face again in English "Society." On the evening of September 10 he invited Sir Augustus to his country home of Winterfold in Cranleigh, near Guildford. He wanted to have a long private talk about strategy on the case, and before Sir Augustus's arrival he prepared yet another "opinion," which reads:

The person who sent Allies several times to Cleveland St, whom Allies saw in Hill Street and from whom Allies received Postal Orders was undoubtedly L.A.S. This evidence is independent altogether of the identification in Piccadilly and of the admission made to Newlove and I note further that a description corresponding as I understand with that of L.A.S. has been given by the witnesses Barber and Swinscow and Thickbroom and Perkins.

If it be the fact that Allies has for some time past been receiving money from L.A.S. and that his mother knew the money came from that person (although her knowledge is not evidence) the truth of Allies' story is in my opinion strongly confirmed. . . . [I]n my opinion the proper course is to issue Summons on sworn information against such persons as can be identified, including L.A.S. for an offence under Section XI of the Criminal Law Amendment Act 1885. There is not in my opinion any sufficient evidence of conspiracy to justify proceedings. In my judgement some communication must be made to the Military Authorities.

Sir Augustus was not entirely happy with the new opinion — he still thought that a warrant should be issued for Somerset's arrest — but felt it was a move in the right direction. On the next day, Sir Augustus forwarded the Attorney General's revised opinion (his third) to Secretary Matthews with an accompanying letter, saying that Sir Richard was ready to take responsibility for directing the action but felt that the decision to obtain a summons should be brought to the Home Secretary's notice "so that you . . . may have the opportunity of conferring with him yourself." The DPP also enclosed a draft of the note that, he proposed, should be sent to Lord Arthur Somerset's military superiors at the War Office after a summons had been obtained.

[70]

On Thursday, September 12, Matthews wrote back to the DPP saying that he had read the "additional papers" and "I cannot say they have altered my opinion and I have written to the AG [Attorney General] to tell him what I think." Sir Richard Webster promptly crumbled again. No summons was applied for; no note was sent to the War Office.

Sir Augustus by now was coming as close as a reserved Victorian gentleman could to frothing at the mouth. He was under some private stress as his son had fallen ill, which meant that he was obliged to spend more of his time away from the office at his own country home, the Manor House, in Market Lavington, Wiltshire. The day-to-day running of the case had been taken over by his diligent assistant, the Honorable Hamilton Cuffe, but Sir Augustus was becoming concerned about the strategic implications of the whole affair. The reputation of his department was at stake and the bloodhounds in the press were sniffing around. The squalid prospect of his office becoming the subject of political controversy began to loom. It was a very worrying situation.

On Sunday, September 15, Sir Augustus devoted his day of rest in Market Lavington to writing a bitter memorandum to Sir Richard Webster. Effectively, he disassociated his department from the entire conduct of the case so far. As it is probably the most important single document in the papers that have recently become available, it merits extensive quotation. It starts in a controlled enough fashion but towards the end the syntax, reflecting the mounting emotion of the author, tends to disintegrate:

I have no apprehension that either the Secretary of State [Matthews] or that you as Attorney General will allow the responsibility of which you cannot relieve me nor can I relieve myself — excepting by distinctly disclaiming, as I now do, most respectfully but most decidedly any agreement with the *opinion* that the evidence now in our possession does not justify or call for the prosecution of LAS.

I acquiesce in your view as expressed in your memo of the 10th inst that a summons charging LAS with offences under Section XI of the Criminal Law Amendment Act — accompanied by a communication to the War Office in terms of my letter to the Secretary of State for War, which is now before the Home Secretary, may be sufficient in the interests of public justice. But my own opinion is that LAS ought to be charged and proceeded against by warrant for conspiring with Hammond with respect to the boy Allies — as Newlove, Veck and Hammond have been charged with respect to the boy Wright.

I think in the interests of public justice this charge ought to be preferred. For if it is not — the evidence of Allies as to the statement made by Hammond to him when he took the letter written by LAS at 19 Hill Street to 19 Cleveland Street and Hammond admitted him "as a friend of Mr Brown's" would be excluded.

In my opinion there is at present direct legal and overwhelming moral evidence against LAS for conspiracy to procure and [word unclear] . . . Allies to commit the felony — in addition to the evidence of the offences under the Criminal Law Amendment Act. There is at present *some* evidence of the same description against Ripley and Cpt M Barber — and that it is my duty as Director of Public Prosecutions (unless otherwise directed by the Attorney-General) having undertaken at the direction of the Sec. of State the prosecution of Newlove and Hammond on the charge of conspiracy — to *include* in that prosecution any other person or persons to whom the evidence already obtained points — as it clearly does to Ripley and Cpt M.B. as conspirators with Newlove and Hammond.

[T]he moral effect of [the evidence] leaves no reasonable doubt that LAS was a frequent visitor at 19 Cleveland Street *for immoral purposes*. The public scandal involved in a criminal charge against a man in his position in society is undoubted — but in my opinion the public scandal in declining to prefer such a charge — and in permitting such a man to hold Her Majesty's Commission and to remain in English Society is much greater.

In my opinion the attempt to avoid such publicity — even if such attempt was justifiable — which in my judgement it is not — must absolutely fail — and the public scandal will then be infinitely aggravated.

Whatever may be said, and much may be said — as to the public policy of allowing *private* persons — being full-grown men to indulge their unnatural tastes — in private — or in such a way as not necessarily to come to public knowledge — in my judgement; the circumstances of this case demand the intervention of those whose *duty* it is to enforce the law and protect the children of respectable parents taken into the service of the public, as these unfortunate boys have been, from being made the victims of the unnatural lusts of full-grown men — and no consideration of public scandal — owing to the position in society or sympathy with the family of the offender should militate against this *paramount duty*.

I feel sure that you will understand and the Sec of State will understand that in trying clearly to express my own views I do so with the greatest deference to his and your own — and in the confident assurance that however we may differ in opinions — we have the same object — to do our duty to the public.

Having thus relieved his feelings, Sir Augustus despatched the memorandum to Cuffe to pass on to the Attorney General. Cuffe was frankly alarmed by its contents, though he also considered that any measure short of the issue of a warrant for Lord Arthur Somerset's arrest would be useless — "a summons is like giving him notice to get away, if in England." Even so, he felt that the DPP's memorandum might stiffen attitudes in a situation that was, he thought, still fluid. Also there was another factor that the DPP might want to consider. He had picked up a spectacular rumor of which

Arthur Newton, the solicitor for the defendants in the case, was the presumed author. "I am *told*" Cuffe wrote in a letter dated September 16, "that Newton has boasted that if we go on a very distinguished person will be involved (P.A.V.). I don't mean to say that for one instant credit it — but in such a case as this one never knows what may be said, be concocted or be true —"

It is the first reference, either in the public or private papers on the case, to the possibility that Prince Albert Victor, Heir Presumptive to the Throne, might be either involved in or dragged into the case. Sir Augustus was evidently shaken by this intelligence. But although his letter from Market Lavington back to Cuffe hinted darkly at the thought that their political masters might have been holding something back, he stuck solidly to his previous position on the case:

We must bear in mind that the Home Secretary may know, or may have information which may lead him to believe that he knows more than we do — also that Mr Newton the Solicitor may know *more* or may believe that he knows *more* than we know. He [Newton] is a dangerous man and he may — or his clients may make utterly *false* accusations against others . . . with respect to whom so far as our information goes — or the *descriptions* given by the boys — there is no shadow of grounds for imputation. Still such imputation may be made. We must not lose sight of such a contingency but whether anything will be gained by abstaining from including LAS in the charge — *with the evidence we have against him* — is a serious question.

The DPP firmly instructed Cuffe to pass on his memorandum to the Attorney General as originally requested. Sir Augustus clearly felt that if there was going to be a cover-up he would like to have it on record that he was not in it.

For those like the Attorney General who favored the policy of minimum public fuss, there was still the hurdle of the Veck and Newlove trial to be surmounted. No mention of Lord Arthur Somerset or any other notables had been made in their indictment, but if the defendants pleaded not guilty there might be a lot of embarrassing publicity, and the possibility of the wrong names slipping out in evidence. The main indictment listed seventeen counts against the defendants (and Hammond in absentia). The first six charged all three with procuring the boys — Thickbroom, Swinscow, Perkins, Barber, Wright and Allies — to commit "divers acts of gross indecency with certain other persons." They were further charged with "conspiracy" to procure the boys "feloniously, wickedly and against the order of nature to commit and perpetrate the detestable and abominable crime of buggery not to be named among Christians and against the peace." Two more counts charged Veck and Hammond with procuring a person "unknown" for acts of "gross indecency"; and the last two counts charged Veck with committing "gross indecency" with Allies and George Barber. A supplementary indictment, of four counts, charged Newlove with two acts of indecency with Wright, and two with Swinscow. Even given the hesitancy of the press about reporting details in cases of this type, there seemed to be no way of avoiding some publicity when the case was heard at the Central Criminal Court.

On September 17, the defense came up with the offer of a deal. Veck's counsel, Mr. C. F. Gill, approached the Treasury counsel, Mr. Avory, and indicated that his client was prepared to plead guilty to the last two counts — misdemeanors — but would not plead guilty to the other fifteen involving the more serious charges of conspiracy, and asked that those charges be dropped. Avory promptly put the suggestion up for comment by his superiors. Neither Cuffe nor Sir Augustus would give an opinion, but the Attorney General was located at his country home in Cranleigh. On the morning of September 18, he telegraphed his instruction to Cuffe: "If both parties plead guilty do not proceed with charges of conspiracy unless counsel strongly advises." The deal was done.

At four o'clock that same afternoon, Veck and Newlove appeared at the Old Bailey before the Recorder, Sir Thomas Chambers, with their guilty pleas — Newlove to the first thirteen counts in the indictment, Veck to the last two. The other charges were formally dropped. Henry Bodkin Poland, Q.C., assisted by Mr. Avory, put the DPP's case. The absence of Hammond was lamented. The recorder sentenced Newlove to four months' penal servitude and Veck to nine months. Arthur Newton, the defendants' solicitor, seemed mightily pleased with the day's work. It was all over in less than an hour and there were no reporters in court — the case had not been set down in the official court list and, without being alerted, most reporters did not bother to wait around for guilty pleas. Cuffe, who was in court, thought the sentences were absurd and sent a sardonic portrait of the trial to Sir Augustus in the country: "The Recorder said hardly anything and the only reason for the ridiculous sentences that can be drawn from what he said was that by pleading guilty they have saved him the trouble of reading the depositions."

Cuffe's engagement that evening was more productive. As soon as the trial was over he hurried down to Cranleigh for dinner with the Attorney General. Sir Richard Webster was going through another agonizing reappraisal but, more importantly, he told Cuffe that the Home Secretary, Henry Matthews, now shared the opinion that Lord Arthur Somerset should be charged. Matthews had made one condition: before he could consent to proceedings being instituted he must have a chance to communicate with Lord Salisbury. Sir

Richard told Cuffe that he was expecting to hear from the Home Secretary or the Prime Minister at any moment. He was distressed by the difficulties of his situation but was prepared to shoulder responsibility once word came through.

On the following day the faithful Cuffe wrote to Sir Augustus, who was still in Market Lavington, relating the most recent thoughts of the Attorney General. By this stage even the DPP's department had given up trying to fathom who precisely had responsibility for what was going on. All they knew was that it was not theirs. Cuffe comforted his superior with the thought: "Whether the AG is personally responsible or whether the Home Secretary or LS [Salisbury] — or the Cabinet are responsible all responsibility is taken off your shoulders. . . ." The letter had a cautionary postscript: "I gather that what the AG told me about Lord Salisbury and the Home Secretary is really for you and me only — and that as regards Matthews we are not supposed to know *yet* what his views are or that he is in correspondence with Lord Salisbury."

It might not yet amount to a criminal conspiracy in law, but the criminal lawyers were becoming extremely conspiratorial.

Shortly after two o'clock on the afternoon of September 25, Algernon Edward Allies received an unexpected visitor. He had been under police protection for over a month and was getting thoroughly bored with the whole business. He might be the most lethal potential witness against Lord Arthur Somerset in the case that was currently disturbing the Prime Minister of Great Britain, but for him personally life was very dull. After the business of giving evidence against Newlove and Veck had been disposed of, Allies was thrown back on the resources of the Rose Coffee House in Hounsditch. It did not have much to offer in the way of diversion for a young man used to the company of gentlemen of "quality." Allies, in consequence, was happy to experience anything that might break the monotony. Besides, the visitor was an agreeable young man with an intriguing proposition.

So intriguing, in fact, that Allies felt obliged to inform his protector, Inspector Abberline, of its details later that same afternoon. Abberline in turn felt obliged to rush Allies round to the DPP's office in the Treasury and get it in writing. The visitor never left his name, but Allies remembered him distinctly:

He was tall and fair — about 25 — dressed like a gentleman with a thin light moustache — with light trousers — light spats and a black jacket and waistcoat and a high hat.

He came upstairs by himself to the dining room where I was. There was another gentleman whom I don't know at dinner at that time. The person said to me "Mr Allies?" I said "Yes" — He then said he would like to speak to me for a minute. I took him up into the sitting room where no one else was. He then said "I've come to persuade you to go away." I said "Well, I must refer you to Insp. Abberline." He said "If you go away to America you shall be found everything — clothing and everything you want — and I will give the Captain about £15 to give you when you get there to go on with." I said I would go, and told him I should want underlinen, two suits, a pair of boots and a hat. He said "All right" — and took a piece of paper out of his pocket book, and wrote down the articles I wanted. He said it would be all right. I asked him how I should get on when I got there. He said "Oh unless you can get work you will be allowed £1 a week." I asked him where he came from and at first he would not tell me. Afterwards I remarked that Mr Newton seemed to be very much against the witnesses — and then he said "You must not take any notice of that — that is where I have come from." He then asked me to meet him this evening at 9 o'clock at the corner of Tottenham Court Road outside the

A.1. public house to go to Liverpool tonight — and he would get my clothing there — and see me off to-morrow for America. I agreed to meet him — and I asked him to let me have the money to get a shirt, collar and tie — and he gave me 6/– and then left — I then went at once to Insp Abberline and told him — and he brought me here. The man told me that he had been down to my home in the country the day before.

Subsequently, Allies recalled the young man saying to him: "The reason we wanted to get you away is that you should not give your evidence against you know who."

At nine o'clock that same evening Allies kept his appointment with the young man in the light spats in Tottenham Court Road. Inspector Abberline, accompanied by P.C. Hanks, watched over the encounter from a discreet distance. The mysterious young man hailed a hansom cab and both he and Allies climbed in. Abberline and Hanks hailed another cab and set off in hot pursuit. It was a short enough journey, ending in familiar surroundings for all concerned. The young man stopped the cab outside the Marlborough Head, a public house opposite the Marlborough Street police court and the offices of the solicitor, Arthur Newton. At the public house, the two policeman saw Augustus De Gallo, Newton's part-time inquiry agent. And Hanks (though not Abberline) was positive he saw Newton himself abruptly walking away from the pub with the tall, fair-haired man as soon as they arrived on the scene. Both policemen moved in on the young man in the light spats. He said that his name was Henry Taylerson, that he was managing clerk to the solicitor Arthur Newton, and that he would not answer any further questions. Abberline took Allies back under his protection.

The issue seemed pretty clear to the police. On the following day Commissioner Monro wrote to the DPP's office requesting permission to arrest Taylerson for conspiracy to pervert the course of justice.

Cuffe, however, still holding the DPP fort while his boss was away in the country, was not nearly so confident. He was not now positive whether Allies would ever be required as a witness. Attorney General Sir Richard Webster already seemed to be regretting his bold assumption of "responsibility" for charging Lord Arthur Somerset after the trial of Newlove and Veck. A few hours before he heard of Taylerson's encounter with Allies, Cuffe had been instructed by the Attorney General to send all the papers on the case off to Lord Halsbury, the Lord Chancellor and, as such, the highest politico-legal authority in the land. Cuffe duly complied, though he told Sir Augustus privately that he thought the further delay imposed by this enterprise was "indefensible." The chances of Lord Halsbury recommending any course of action offensive to the Prime Minister were — at best — no better than even. He also happened to be on holiday in Scotland. In short, Cuffe was in no position to make a rapid decision though he was fully alert to the danger. Cuffe reported the attempted abduction of Allies to the Attorney General with the caution that "It is possible similar offers will be made to others . . . and, if ultimately instructed to proceed, we may find ourselves without witnesses. . . . [T]hose who are in danger have every reason for putting them out of the way and plenty of money to do it."

Before the authorities could capitalize on the alert sleuthing of Abberline and Hanks, Arthur Newton came back with an attack calculated to put them further on the defensive. His letter of September 27 to the DPP's office put the encounter between Allies and Taylerson in a radically different light. The police were the double-dyed villains of the piece. Newton, seemingly, could scarcely contain his outrage:

This boy [Allies] had been kept by Inspector Abberline and PC Hanks in a small Coffee House in Hounsditch in a state of duress being threatened by these officers and commanded not to leave the place and they have even told him what to say in letters which he wrote to his own Father.

Acting upon instructions (which we have in writing) received from his Father, with whom he was living prior to his giving evidence in the case (against Veck and Newlove), our Managing Clerk called on Wednesday last at Hounsditch and saw this boy and told him that it was his Father's wish to remove him from the objectionable associations into which he had most unfortunately fallen and that his Father had given instructions to make arrangements for him to return home with a view to his being given a fresh start abroad.

The boy stated that he most anxious to get away from the objectionable surroundings but that he was in a state of terror and fright owing to the threats made by the Police. He accordingly on the evening of Wednesday last met our Managing Clerk, he was followed by Insp. Abberline and PC Hanks who took the boy into custody and actually had the audacity to threaten to detain our Managing Clerk.

We can hardly imagine that this course has been carried out by your instructions, sanction, or authority, but with a view to avoiding the necessity of taking any unpleasant steps in the matter we ask you to be so good as to give us an appointment when Mr Allies can in our company take possession of his son, as of course we are anxious to avoid any collision with the Police by going again to fetch him from where he now is without having communicated with you who had the conduct of the case.

Mr Allies is coming here tomorrow morning and we should be much obliged if you would kindly let us have an appointment in the course of today when our Client can fetch his son as he had written bitterly complaining of the way in which he is treated, not being supplied with clothes of his own, so as to render it absolutely impossible for him to go away.

We may say that it is perfectly plain that when the Police were not present with their influence upon him that he was perfectly anxious and willing to go away but that he was so overawed.

It was an exceptionally feisty letter to send to a public prosecutor, especially from a young solicitor who claimed to be representing no more than the parental concern of a poor East Anglian coachman. The outrage was clearly synthetic, but the letter contained enough half-truths to be worrying (Allies,, subsequently, admitted that he had rather fancied the idea of going to America, though he denied the allegations about his being pressured by the police). Cuffe sent a letter to Newton denying the allegations and warning him that Allies might yet be required as a witness against Hammond and that anyone who was a party to his leaving the country could be prosecuted. The DPP's information was that Allies's father was in no position to sponsor a transatlantic crossing for his son, and he therefore found it "difficult to avoid the inference that such funds were to be furnished from other sources." (This was no bad inference as Allies's father had to ask Newton to send him a postal order for £1 before he could undertake the expense of coming to London to see Algernon.)

Cuffe established that Allies did not, at that stage, want to see his father and forwarded his exchange of letters with Newton to the Lord Chancellor. It seemed as much as he could do until someone, somewhere, decided what to do on the main issue of the evidence against Lord Arthur Somerset.

As far as the police were concerned the DPP's ostensibly limp response to the attempted abduction of Allies seemed like further evidence of incompetence. Scotland Yard was also worried about the possibility of completely losing track of Hammond, who had been tailed from Paris to Halenzy in Belgium. When bureaucracies reach a certain level of frustration they tend to get "leaky"; the Metropolitan Police was no exception.

On Saturday, September 28, the first detailed story on the case — clearly based on police sources — appeared in *The North London Press*, a saucy, radical weekly, with a circulation of 4,500. Its editor, Ernest Parke, was only twenty-nine years old but knew what the customers wanted. There was nothing like a bit of peer-basing for building circulation, and the issue of the last week in September was a corker. So good, in fact, that even the potent details of the Cleveland Street affair failed to lead the scandal page. The main story, lifted from a Scottish paper, concerned the Earl of Galloway, Lord Salisbury's brother-in-law and a former Lord High Commissioner to the General Assembly of the Church of Scotland. Lord Galloway faced a charge of using "lewd and libidinous practices" against a ten-year-old girl in Dumfries, and Scotland's Procurator-Fiscal was gathering evidence. ("I saw a man holding a little girl on the wall" stated a Miss Moffat; "I ran forward and exclaimed, 'For shame, you old blackguard! What have you been doing?' The man replied, 'We have been gathering Brambles.' ")

The report on the Cleveland Street case had fewer ripe details but more potential for growth. After describing what happened at Newlove's and Veck's trial — that "practically took place in secret" — the story commented on how Hammond had "levanted" in highly suspicious circumstances. *The North London Press* claimed that it had "the names of men highly placed in the nobility who patronised the house. . . . Amongst them were the heir of a duke, the younger son of another duke, and an officer holding command in the Southern District." It was ready to produce the names if necessary. The case was made all the more dreadful by virtue of the "scandalous sentences"; a Hackney minister had not long before been sentenced to life imprisonment for a similar crime. It was clear from the internal evidence of the article that Parke had — or had been shown — a copy of Newlove's original statement to P.C. Hanks (mentioning Lord Arthur Somerset, the Earl of Euston, and a Colonel Ueavons). Official security on the internal documents of the case had finally collapsed. On the following day, *Reynolds's Newspaper* gave Ernest Parke's local "scoop" national prominence by reprinting the *North London Press* article in full.

Cuffe, in the DPP's office, did not seem too alarmed by the breach of security; in one way he was rather pleased — it might finally move those in high places. He sent the clipping to the Lord Chancellor in Braemar and wrote to Sir Augustus Stephenson: "Nothing from the Lord Chancellor apparently! However I feel pretty sure that if nothing else will, those newspaper extracts which I have sent on will produce some action. There can be no doubt lots of people know the names — and there are some MPs who would delight in the case."

On October 2, Inspector Abberline also made what seemed a very sensible move by serving subpoenas on Allies and the other boys to appear as witnesses against Hammond at the next session of the Old Bailey, starting on October 21. This would give time for renewed attempts to have Hammond extradited and remove any arguments from Arthur Newton or anybody else about the necessity for Allies's staying in the country. Abberline did not then know that, even as he was serving the subpoenas, Newton was making final arrangements that would place Hammond six thousand miles away from the original scene of his crime.

❧❧ FIVE ❧❧

Packing the Velvet Curtains

Charles Hammond's odyssey since the morning of July 5, when he furtively slipped away from 19 Cleveland Street carrying a large black portmanteau, had been exceptionally bleak. He was frantically busy with his travel arrangements, and also a prey to very understandable doubts about his "friends" — the phrase he usually employed to refer to the society world of influence and ready cash. Could they be trusted? Would they deliver the money he needed to keep him on the move and out of jail — "*my* money," as it became in his mind?

And there was a worse fear, one that can never have left him. Every knock on the door, every chance jostling on a crowded station might be the preliminary to arrest. He knew that they had issued a warrant for him and that Inspector Abberline's men from Scotland Yard were hard on his heels.

Worst of all there was Mr. John Phillips of the Post Office Confidential Inquiry Bureau, who had become his shadow. A very intense personal element entered into the strange relationship of these two, Phillips the hunter and Hammond the prey.

Phillips, in decent black bowler and serge suit, was one of the "bulldog breed" Kipling's schoolboys were taught to admire as they were trained to administer the empire. He never let go; all the more so now when his natural tenacity was reinforced by his sense of duty to the Post Office. Hammond had corrupted "The Service," as Phillips called the post; he was a loathsome creature who threatened everything Phillips held sacred. And now, tantalizingly near but still protected by circumstances Phillips did not fully comprehend, Hammond led him to Paris, which the middle-class English thought of as "the City of Sin."

From Cleveland Street Hammond had stopped briefly at his brother's house in Gravesend. There he found a companion in distress, one who would fulfill his emotional (and also practical) needs. When he left for France the black portmanteau was in the hands of one Bertie Ames, a working-class lad from Mile End in East London's dockland to whom history owes a modest debt. For throughout this period of intense pressure, Ames became Hammond's official scribe. The brothel-keeper had many handy attainments but the "Three R's" were not among them.

Since good communications were now so important for Hammond's survival — the telegraph offices provided his lifeline — having Ames on hand to take dictation became a crucial factor. The fact that it *was* dictation, literally word for word, has had the uncanny effect of preserving the very character of Hammond's voice. Under pressure he became a bit uncertain about grammar, especially when John Phillips and the men from Scotland Yard were getting really close.

Most of Hammond's continental correspondence has survived. It fell into the hands of Ernest Parke, the resourceful editor of *The North London Press* — presumably as a result of an early enterprise in "checkbook journalism" — and he, in turn, after running some extracts in the newspaper, handed the letters on to the Director of Public Prosecutions. The whole series gives a remarkable insight not only into Hammond's immediate troubles but also into the private life and family concerns of a typical Victorian homosexual "Madame."

Hammond was not a man to waste time when he was in trouble, and by July 10 he had arrived in Paris and gone like an arrow to the heart of the red-light area which, with the Place des Abbesses as its apex, and the Place Blanche and the Place Pigalle as the other sides, forms a triangle. Today, as in 1889, the narrow streets of this urban hamlet running north off the Boulevard de Clichy are a haven for Montmartre prostitutes and their protectors in the criminal *milieu*. Hammond, knowing the *quartier* from his adventures in Paris as a young man, must have felt at home. For John Phillips, who was close behind, the atmosphere of seething low-life, clip-joints and cabarets, must have confirmed his worst imaginings.

Less than a week after leaving Cleveland Street the first letter reporting Hammond's arrival and his address — care of a certain "Madame de Foissard" at 8, Passage des Abbesses — was on its way to Mrs. Hammond. Her husband was by now secure enough in his foreign lodgings to indulge in some domestic nagging. There had been some question of her joining him — she was French, after all, and knew her way around — but Hammond was having none of this. "It seems to me that you want to spend all our money," he dictated. She was to watch out for Veck, a weak but important link whom Hammond needed to keep in with but could not find it in his heart to trust. "Be very careful what you say to him," Caroline is warned.

Meanwhile Hammond was busy establishing communications with Veck and sent an SOS for cash. On July 13, he again dictated a letter to Caroline: "Let me know by return of post how much money Veck has been able to obtain. If he has not got what I asked for, I will write to our friends." The next day, July 14, he sent another letter to his wife, far too preoccupied to make any reference to the *quatorze juillet* celebrations going on around him on France's most important national holiday. He was not in a frivolous mood.

"Mr. Veck has written to tell me that me friends will come to see me in Paris to arrange them money. I expect £20 by next Saturday."

This was the first note of warning from Hammond — he had given an ultimatum to the "friends" via Veck and "their" representative, Arthur Newton, the solicitor. At this point Hammond's forebodings were confirmed — there was trouble with Veck and it seemed that Florence, his wife's sister, had quarreled with this self-styled man of the cloth. Hammond was in a querulous mood by July 17, and Ames had to do a long secretarial stint.

My dear Caroline — a few lines to tell you that I have written to Mr Ripley and ask them to find everything out for me, as I do not think things are so bad as what people tell you.

For if they wanted to find your mother or Florence they could have followed the furniture and they would soon found [*sic*] you. You must remember that whatever was done was not done in our house it was done in the Post Office. I think you have been very silly to let Florence or yourself fall out with Mr Veck. You ought to have been friends with him until all the trouble had blown over. I had a letter from him this morning. He tells me that Florence insulted him, and has not told him anything, so he has not known what to do about money for me. You remember I told you to take him to Gravesend with you, for you know he has got all the addresses of my friends. I have written to ask him to come over to France to see me. He wants me to come to London, but that I shall not do until I can see everything is all right.

He continues on a domestic tack which led a *North London Press* commentator, examining the evidence nearly four months later, to conclude: "Hammond at this time contemplated returning to England." This was a misreading of a cautious man; Hammond calculated no such risky course. His congenital fussiness exaggerated the landlady/family man aspect of his character and his furniture was close to his heart.

We hear no more of "Mr. Ripley," who is presumably the same as "E.G. Ripley," a name which is mentioned in the DPP's memoranda as someone who, like Hammond and Veck, should have been charged with conspiracy in connection with the brothel. But then Caroline, unwilling to hang around long enough for someone to think of tracing the furniture removers, arrived in Paris herself. On July 23 they were writing joint letters home, but still in the clerkly handwriting of young Ames. They had also moved house again, from the seedy end of Montmartre to a quiet suburb where a relative of Mrs. Hammond had a house.

John Phillips, the patient Post Office shadow, had naturally followed the motley entourage, and to add to their discomfort Hammond's "friends" had failed to come through with the promised cash. The situation became so bad that

Hammond was reduced on July 23 to sending a letter to their son Charles. The boy was only nine and a half, a tender age for the delicate mission his father had in mind. He had to reestablish communications with Veck, who himself had been swapping addresses, and also, it transpired, names as well.

My dear Son, — A few lines to you to let you know that we are all right, and ask you to send us a long letter and tell me how things are going on. Tell your Uncle not to tell Mr Veck that your mama is over here with me. Ask Uncle to write to him, and ask him why he does not come over to see me or send me any money. I think there must be something wrong. As he has changed his name and living under the name of George Barber, at 2, Howland Street, Tottenham Court Road, London. If we do not get any news me and mama think of coming back. Ask your uncle to send me a newspaper if there is anything in it.

Your loving father and mother.

It was asking a lot of a child and Charles evidently fell down on a difficult job. Hammond, with another letter six days later, launched into a dignified reprimand worthy of the most upright Victorian paterfamilias — Charles had, moreover, spent the sum of 8s 3d on nails, which his father said was too extravagant. There was an urgent postscript: "Do not forget that if someone comes and asks for me, there is no Mr Hammond, only a Mrs Hammond and she is at the seaside."

It was a very genteel alibi; the seaside was a respectable place to be at the end of July. It may have been the prospect of impending holidays and possible delay that provoked John Phillips to send a telegram to his superiors in the Post Office early in August. He needed the support of someone who would carry weight with the French police who could complete the arrangements with them about Hammond's extradition. Conscientiously staking out the Hammond family, he was blissfully ignorant that Lord Salisbury had decided against applying for extradition at all. But the Phillips reminder had some effect because on August 8 Inspector Abberline himself arrived.

It was a brief visit, just long enough for Abberline to find that the French police were more interested in their own local vice problem than in the overflow from London. There was nothing to be done without the extradition order; the French authorities were reluctant to bestir themselves without the correct paperwork. Abberline hurried back to London and was replaced by another Scotland Yard man, Inspector Lowe, so John Phillips had a companion to share the surveillance of the Hammond ménage, a chore which dragged on for the rest of the month.

By early September the French authorities were no longer satisfied to wait for the famous extradition order, which they shrewdly deduced had a chimerical quality attached to it implying disagreement or stalemate in London. They decided it would be prudent to let someone else worry about the Hammonds. On September 12 a gendarme served him with an executive order requiring him to leave the country.

They went quietly, probably relieved that the uniform had only heralded expulsion and not arrest. Caroline returned to London; Hammond himself, accompanied by the faithful Ames, made a swift journey to Halenzy in Belgium. Inspector Lowe reported this move to Scotland Yard. Phillips, as always, kept the fugitives in view.

This unrelenting pressure was beginning to affect Hammond's nerves, as his melancholy letter of Sunday, September 22, revealed. It was addressed to his sister-in-law with a fervent plea that she should waste no time in pursuing an earlier message sent to Mr. Newton — and, of course, the "friends":

My dear Florence,
A line to let your know that we are still at the same place. One of the 2 men that followed us from France has gone away and a Belgium [sic] man has come in his place. If we only go across the road from the hotel, they follow us. If I ask any questions, they go and ask the people what I said to them. It makes me feel so ill I can scarcely eat my meals. I wished to god I knew what they are going to do. But I expect they will hunt us about from place to place. I hope poor Caroline is home.

This perfunctory reference to his wife's problems is a preliminary to some more words of paternal advice to young Charles.

Now my dear Charlie be kind and good to your mother and likewise to everybody. Try and learn all you can for you will perhaps help your mother. Stick to your Music for that will be useful by and by so good-bye and god bless you. Dear Florence, try and do all you can to make Caroline as happy as she can be. You must stick to one another and do all you can for each other. For things may soon come to the worst and I may be turned away at a minute's notice and I have but very little money left and traveling is so expensive I wish Mr New ton would send someone over with money at once. . . . I hope you went to Mr Newton and showed him the letter I sent you the other day.
I remain your most Unhappy Brother
Charlie

Hammond's apprehension was fully justified. Inspector Greenham had replaced Inspector Lowe as Scotland Yard's man on the Hammond hunt, and the Belgian police were proving much more accommodating than the French. They made a tantalizing offer to arrest Hammond if they could obtain in advance a high-level assurance from London that a formal request for extradition would be made. The assurance was never given; the DPP still felt that their hands were tied by Lord Salisbury's ruling. Hammond, meanwhile, was close to despair though he could see a glimmer of light at the end of the tunnel. On September 30, he wrote to his wife:

My dear Caroline I have just read your letter about your hardships. Sometimes I wish I were dead and in our coffins. Try & take courage for they cannot touch me where I am. . . . If they give me what I asked for we could all be reunited and everything to do the best we can for each other. . . . I am waiting to see what they are going to give me. They sent me over 30 for my present expenses. I have just read a telegram from them asking me to go nearer to Brussles so as he can come over to see me. I suppose it means to arrange with me about what money I am to have.

The Brussels meeting was a great success, and Hammond and Ames finally managed to give their police escort the slip. On Thursday, October 3, the day that Abberline was rushing around London serving subpoenas on Allies and the other boys to give evidence at Hammond's trial, Hammond wrote a cheerful letter to his wife, full of practical advice about how to prepare for a new life in the New World:

My Dear Caroline, I am in Anvers, under the name Barber, at the Hotel de L'Europe, and am happy to tell you that we have escaped without being followed. After twelve hours hard journey. I must tell you my Solicitor [Newton] met me at Brussels this morning and then we went to his hotel and had a long talk about everything. He wants me to start for America on Saturday by the American Steamer that sails under the American Flag for New York. He said he would pay all expenses for first Class Passage. And give me Three Hundred

Pounds But I refused to take such a little money. I told him he must pay all my Family's Expenses First Class Passage And give me Eight Hundred Pounds to start business with. He asked me how many there was to pay for. I told him there was three of you. So you will only have to pay for Florence's Passages. But if I can get him to pay for Florences passage, I shall try. He will come down and see you. You will know him it is the same one that came on that Sunday at Papa's. So my dear if I go on Saturday which I will telegraph and let you know. You must sell all the things off by Auction. Ted [Hammond's brother in Gravesend] will tell you how to do it. Sell all the Birds. But you must bring Rose [thought to be Hammond's sister] with you when you are ready to come. If you sell the things before you are ready to start after I send you my address from America. You must go & stay for a few days at Ted's. You must buy another large basket like the large one you have got to pack the Bed Linen and Velvet Curtains in and the two yellow silk Pillows. You can pack the best Dresden Vases that are on my Mantle Glass And the few best plates there are the 2 large round ones and the Blue Dresden Dish that hangs on the walls. If Ted can get our Oil Paintings packed nicely I should like him to send them to me later on when I send my address or anything you would like him to keep to send out to us. Ask Ted to ask how much it would cost for the Pianos to come over to America properly packed. They would tell him at one of the Piano shops in High Street. If I go on Saturday I will telegraph to you as soon as I arrive in America.

Hammond wrote still more confidently on the next day:

Friday morning 12.5 am oclock. My Dear Caroline, Just another letter to you to tell you that . . . I expect the solicitor here every minute to tell me if I am to have the Eight Hundred Pounds I shall arrange with him to pay all your passages out as Saloon Passengers. So my dear you will only have to pay for Rose. Of course you can show this to Mr Newton when you see him. Without he refuses to pay for Florence then of course you must. . . . I hope you asked Papa to send you any letters that went there in the name of King or Charles or Hammond. . . . Of course I shall want my money before I sail.

Hammond received his eight hundred pounds and wrote briefly to his wife the next morning: "Saturday 6.30 am oclock. My Dear Caroline, A few lines to let you know we have started for America. Mr Newton wants you to come over in a week but of course if you have not sold your things you must say you cannot come over for a fortnight. . . ."

Practical to the last, Hammond advised his wife to buy ankle-boots in London as they were expensive in America, but she had to be sure to dirty up the soles before packing them to avoid paying customs duty.

On the morning of October 5, Hammonds and Bertie Ames, traveling under the names Mr. Charles and Mr. Arthur Boulton, and accompanied by Mr. Frederick Taylerson, Newton's managing clerk, set sail for New York from Antwerp on the S.S. *Pennland*. The final letter in the archive, to his brother Ted, records their safe arrival in the United States:

On board the S.S. Pennland, New York. My Dear Brother & Sister, A few lines to let you know that we arrived quite safe at New York after a very nice voyage.

I shall leave here to morrow for Adele's at Washington.

This is the address. I send you the copy in case you have forgotten it. Miss Adele Gayet, care of John Staker, 593, Post Box, Seattle, Washington, Territory, America.
I Remain
Your Affectionate
Brother
Charlie.

It was some days before Mr. Phillips, who had spent ten weeks on the Hammond trail, and Inspector Greenham, who had spent three, learned that they had lost their man. On October 6 Commissioner Monro, still under the delusion that Hammond was under observation in Belgium, wrote to the DPP with yet another extradition request. He drew attention to the stigma that would rest on the English police *if* Hammond were allowed to escape.

SIX

"My Lord Gomorrah Smiled"

O ne of the more touching aspects of the Cleveland Street affair was the appealing relationship which developed between Sir Augustus Stephenson, the Director of Public Prosecutions, and his assistant, the Honorable Hamilton Cuffe. Throughout the month of September, the pressures of the case were grueling enough to have disrupted even the most harmonious of professional relationships. And there was an additional stress factor — Stephenson's son was sick, which meant he had a deeper source of continuing worry to contend with. On the one hand he was anxious that no aspect of an increasingly complicated and delicate case should be allowed to slip out of his hands. On the other, his son's illness required him to make frequent visits to his country house at Market Lavington in Wiltshire, ninety-five miles from his Whitehall office where the major decisions had to be taken.

They made up for this geographical problem by constant written communication, a correspondence which survives in the Public Records Office. From it a pattern emerges — one combining a high sense of responsibility and deep mutual comprehension. Although the letters make it clear that both men were typical Victorians insofar as open displays of affection were excluded, the subtle interplay of shared competence and real concern is evident at many levels. The correspondence is a model of reserved grace, revealing a total respect for each man's individual and separate function, and the distance between them.

This gap of rank and responsibility is bridged by a number of gestures which not only indicate the sense each man has of the other as a person, but also help to raise their joint performance.

At the outset Sir Augustus is clearly concerned about Cuffe's ability in a fraught situation and is almost obsessive in his attention to detail. Cuffe on his side obviously senses that his chief is under stress because of the illness in his family and the puzzling behavior of his political superiors. The impression comes through that Cuffe is happy to share the burden of some of the loneliness involved in the DPP's decisions by giving reassurance in an emotional as well as an executive sense. But there is no suggestion of Uriah Heep in that support; Cuffe is at all stages his own man and capable, when circumstances seem to indicate that Sir Augustus is about to overreact, of gently suggesting more moderate courses of action which would still effectively achieve the DPP's godly objectives but in more mysterious ways. The pleasant asides in Cuffe's official letters, indicating concern for the son's progress or sometimes the state of the weather in Sir Augustus's country home in Market Lavington, are more than grace notes. Cuffe is indicating a genuine human sympathy and understanding without in any way trying to suggest that Sir Augustus could escape from the awful loneliness of making hard choices. From mid-September onwards there is a detectable relaxation in the tone of the DPP's replies to Cuffe's letters asking for guidance. Sir Augustus has clearly lost his abiding fear that Cuffe might put a foot wrong and has begun to appreciate that his assistant's sense of direction may in some ways be better than his own. By late September, the DPP finds that his son is well on the way to recovery and wisely decides not to rush back to the office but to take his annual holiday at Lochinch in Scotland, where he could shoot a few grouse and generally unwind by trying his hand at the autumn salmon. There is still plenty of tension in the case, for both men seem to appreciate that the Treasury Solicitor might well be made the scapegoat for the errors and subterfuges of men of more eminence, but there is a new sense of ease in their correspondence, conveying a feeling that whatever might happen in the future both know that a nice balance of passion and responsibility has been achieved through their joint efforts on the case. It is the kind of experience that often creates a bond, and by early October they are communicating with a degree of intimacy that would have been unimaginable six weeks earlier. They are friends as well as colleagues, relaxed in the sense that for them the worst seems to be over.

The fact that copies of all the papers in the case were now with Lord Halsbury, the Lord Chancellor, evidently took a weight off both their minds. They might not agree with the way in which the Lord Chancellor had been drawn into the decision-making process, but now that it was an accomplished fact they could enjoy the accompanying sense of relief that their own direct responsibility was somewhat diminished.

Lord Halsbury himself was also in Scotland shooting grouse but his world did not impinge on that of Sir Augustus Stephenson. The records show no evidence of any official communication between the Lord Chancellor and the DPP, and there was none of an informal nature. Lord Halsbury was in Braemar and seemingly in no hurry to arrive at a decision about whether to recommend the arrest of Lord Arthur Somerset who was after all still "on leave" and out of jurisdiction of Her Majesty's courts of justice. His Lordship perceived no reason for delving too deeply into the massive dossier on a case which could not conceivably improve either his temper or his eye for the birds. Cuffe, writing to Sir Augustus on Friday, October 4, commented rather sardonically on the Lord Chancellor's continued neglect of the papers and commented in passing on an item of news. Lord Arthur Somerset's grandmother, the Dowager Duchess of Beaufort, had just died and was to be buried on the grounds of the family estate in Badminton. "One is almost glad," wrote Cuffe, "that the old Duchess of Beaufort should have died before all this came to light. She was apparently devoted to Lord A.S. who lived at her house in London when not in barracks. . . ."

The tone was that of a man passing on an item of gossip. He could not then know that the event was to be the prelude to the most dramatic stages of the affair and that the royal household would play a central role in determining its development. For Lord Arthur Somerset had also been moved by news of his grandmother's death and was emboldened by the knowledge that Charles Hammond, the all too knowing "Madame" of 19 Cleveland Street, was securely pointed in the direction of the United States. Lord Arthur slipped back into the country in order to pay his last respects and gently test the official atmosphere which would determine his position — if any — in Society.

Scotland Yard viewed his return with ill-concealed fury. To Commissioner Monro and Inspector Abberline, it seemed yet another example of the bland aristocratic insouciance and contempt for the police that they had felt to be the attitude of higher authority from the very beginning. Monro learned of Lord Arthur's return within hours of his arrival on Saturday, October 5. He communicated immediately with Cuffe in a note delivered by special messenger: "I learn on the best authority that LAS is in town. I cannot take steps to arrest without a warrant, and I must leave it to you to say whether I am to have that warrant that it may be executed while the accused is within my jurisdiction."

Once again Cuffe was plunged into the middle of the action without any specific brief. And once again events had climaxed over the weekend, never the best of times for obtaining a decision from any public servant, English or otherwise. Apart from the problems created by timing, the sheer communications difficulties made a speedy response impossible. Lord Halsbury would have to be consulted, almost certainly by telegram, and that would have to be delivered by hand over many miles of desolate track and mountain path. And it was too much for any English gentleman to expect Lord Halsbury to arrive at his decision in the brief intervals between the driven coveys of grouse winging over the guns. Cuffe's automatic first move was to notify Attorney General Sir Richard Webster immediately, by sending a message to his country home at Cranleigh, about thirty miles from London. Cuffe pointed out that he himself had no authority to countenance the warrant requested by Monro. The Attorney General replied by hand the same day, saying that he was in great difficulty as he was himself awaiting the Lord Chancellor's instructions. He suggested that Cuffe should either send an immediate message to Scotland by hand (which would provide maximum security for its contents) or use the telegraph. But if the telegraph were used in the interests of speed, then he urged the need for discretion in its wording. Sir Richard was in favor of using the pseudonym "Brown" for any reference to Lord Arthur Somerset, the assumption being that the Lord Chancellor would immediately perceive the connection from his knowledge of the identity of the "Mr. Brown" in the statements by Allies and the post office boys. Cuffe duly telegraphed on Sunday morning:

The Lord Chancellor
Kinrockit Cottage,
Braemar.
BROWN IS IN ENGLAND. CAN YOU SEND OPINION TO AG OR ME. I WRITE BY TONIGHTS POST. TIME MAY BE OF IMPORTANCE. CUFFE TREASURY.

Cuffe was clearly slightly overawed at the enormity of finding himself having to communicate directly with the Lord Chancellor, especially in a way that implied a certain dilatoriness on Lord Halsbury's part. On the same Sunday evening, Cuffe wrote a careful letter to the Lord Chancellor in which he apologized for the apparent peremptoriness of his earlier telegram. There were good reasons and Cuffe explained them:

"After the failure to put the witness [Algernon] Allies out of the country I am surprised that L.A.S. should have returned and [as] it appeared to me improbable that he would remain any time, that I thought it would not be right to wait until a letter could reach you — which appears to be at the soonest about 5pm tomorrow [Monday]." He went on to say that numerous people in London knew of Lord Arthur Somerset's connection with the case, and that news of the failure of the attempt to spirit away Allies, the chief material witness against him, had reached the ears of Lord Arthur's friends. The innuendo was clear enough: if Halsbury did not respond quickly Lord Arthur Somerset might easily escape justice, probably for good. As a footnote Cuffe added that he had "everything ready to apply for a warrant."

The strain was beginning to tell on Cuffe's syntax as well as his nerves. Nevertheless, he found the time to write yet another letter to Sir Augustus Stephenson which kept his chief fully in the picture and provided an elegant safety valve for his own obviously mounting tension and sense of anticipation. Cuffe explained why he had been forced to drop the idea of contacting Lord Halsbury at Braemar by special messenger. The journey via Blair Athol, for example, involved seven hours by coach after a long train journey. On balance, Cuffe had decided that the telegraph was the better method and the men in the Charing Cross Post Office had been most helpful. They had not promised, but had indicated that "as it is a government telegram," delivery might be possible that same day. Cuffe mentioned the possibility that excessive reverence for the Sabbath at the delivery end might defeat the best efforts of the willing public servants at Charing Cross. "Scotchmen on a Sunday," wrote Cuffe, "may be hard to move."

Scotland Yard, in anticipation of a positive response from higher authority, was already moving into gear. The job of shadowing Lord Arthur Somerset was given to P.C. Luke Hanks, who was by now deeply involved in the case at a personal as well as a professional level. Happy to be in at what seemed like the kill, Hanks spent the weekend traveling to Badminton, where he had every intention of arresting Lord Arthur at his grandmother's graveside if necessary.

Lord Halsbury's reply to Cuffe's telegram arrived at the DPP's office in the Treasury at 4:30 P.M. Monday afternoon. It had been sent at 12:50 P.M. from Braemar. The timing was evidence that Lord Halsbury appreciated the urgency, but the wording was cryptic in the extreme: "OPINION GOES TONIGHTS POST. CANNOT RECOMMEND AS TO B UNLESS CORROBORATION OF A."

Cuffe quickly deduced that "B" referred to "Brown," the alias for Lord Arthur Somerset, and that "A" referred to the crucial evidence of Algernon Allies. Cuffe wisely interpreted the telegram as an instruction to stay his hand at least until the Lord Chancellor's opinion arrived, hopefully in the next day's mailbag. But the next day, Tuesday, October 8, came and went with no sign of the opinion. At Badminton, the Dowager Duchess was finally laid to rest in the family vaults, her grandson, Lord Arthur Somerset, conspicuous among the mourners. Less conspicuous among the fringe observers of the scene was a tight-faced P.C. Hanks, still waiting instructions to arrest and conscious that the opportunity for it was slipping away. He had telegraphed his superiors at lunchtime, requesting permission to effect the arrest of Lord Arthur. There had been no reply.

The Lord Chancellor's opinion arrived on Cuffe's desk in the Treasury building on the morning of Wednesday, October 9, and the reason for the delay in delivery was immediately obvious. The Lord Chancellor, casual to the last, had addressed it to "Cuffe Esq, Law Office, Home Office." The contents of the opinion itself seemed to suggest an equally slipshod approach to the accumulated evidence, though it contained some fine phrasing:

[104]

1 ABOVE Henry
Labouchere, Radical MP
for Northampton and editor
of *Truth*, was a leading
political investigator of the
Cleveland Street affair.

2 RIGHT Henry Asquith,
Liberal MP, acted as
defense attorney for the
journalist, Ernest Parke,
who was jailed for his
Cleveland Street "revela-
tions." Later Asquith
became Prime Minister and
Earl of Oxford.

3 ABOVE LEFT Lord Salisbury was Conservative Prime Minister at the time of the Cleveland Street affair and chief political architect of the Establishment's cover-up.

4 ABOVE Sir Richard Webster, Attorney-General, defended the government's Cleveland Street case in the House of Commons.

5 LEFT Henry Matthews, as Home Secretary, had ministerial responsibility for the police's handling of the case. Later he was created Viscount Llandaff.

6 LEFT W. H. Smith was both a bookstore proprietor and First Lord of the Treasury, the government department that examined the legal aspects of the Cleveland Street case.

7 BELOW William Thomas Stead, editor of *The Pall Mall Gazette* and exponent of the "new journalism," was the first to break news of an aristocratic connection with the homosexual brothel in Cleveland Street that employed off-duty telegraph boys.

8 LEFT Sir Henry "Hanging" Hawkins sentenced one of the journalistic investigators of the affair to prison. Later he was elevated to peerage as Baron Brampton.

9 BELOW "Bertie" (the Prince of Wales, later Edward VII), in a study taken in 1890, wears one of his favorite uniforms. He acted as chief royal architect of the Cleveland Street cover-up.

I have very carefully considered the matter and I am unable on the present materials to advise further proceedings. . . . The offence alleged to have been committed is an offence created by the recent statute and only a misdemeanour. The punishments already inflicted seem to me very inadequate are likely to do harm than good. If as is alleged in the papers, the social position of some of the parties will make a great sensation this will give very wide publicity and consequently will spread very extensively written matter of the most revolting and mischievous kind, the spread of which I am satisfied will produce enormous evil. If a successful prosecution could be reasonably looked for, and if the sentence could be penal servitude for life, or something which by its terrible severity would strike terror into such wretches as the keeper of such a house or his adult customers; I should take a different view, but, as I have pointed out, the only offence alleged is the new misdemeanour and at present I doubt very much the success of a prosecution.

If material corroboration of Allies can be obtained . . . then the question will remain purely one of policy in the public interest, but at present I see no corroboration whatever and though in structures of law this is a question for the jury and not one of law yet I do not think there is a judge upon the Bench who would allow a jury to convict upon such a charge without some real corroboration of the accomplices in the alleged offence.

If untainted witnesses can be obtained that any of the parties charged were seen going into or coming out of the house in Cleveland Street this I think would be real corroboration but as it is the sole evidence offered "has to be" tainted with the very guilt which is in question here and not to be relied on alone for an accusation made on the responsibility of the Public Prosecutor.

Cuffe's muted sense of irony must have been tickled by Lord Halsbury's implication that the Public Prosecutor's office should not trifle in cases of misdemeanor, his reason for not pressing the charge. Cuffe knew better than anybody that if the case had been originally dealt with as trivial it would never have come to the DPP's office and Lord Arthur Somerset would have been arrested, charged by the police, brought to trial and probably found guilty long since. Cuffe had enough sense of self-preservation not to make this point in his written report on the Lord Chancellor's opinion for Attorney General Sir Richard Webster. He did, however, stress large areas of disagreement with the reasons given by Lord Halsbury, remarking that untainted evidence — *i.e.*, testimony from persons free of any suspicion of complicity in the offenses — did exist in the form of P.C. Sladden's reports on Lord Arthur Somerset's comings and goings at 19 Cleveland Street. He also indicated that there were at least three other people acquainted with the brothel who might be taken to identify Lord Arthur (presumably in what was threatening to become a somewhat overcrowded congregation of mourners at Badminton). Having done his duty vis-à-vis the Attorney General, Cuffe again wrote to Sir Augustus Stephenson, and began to speak his mind in a most uncivil-servant-like fashion. "We are told not to speak evil of dignitaries but the temptation to do so is sometimes very great." Cuffe reiterated his point about there being ample untainted evidence, and commented sardonically that "If identification by respectable witnesses is a condition . . . it comes to saying there shall be no prosecution. People do not do these things in the presence of persons of respectability as a rule." He then passed on an intriguing snippet of information from the police. Commissioner Monro had just sent round a note saying that Lord Arthur's Commanding Officer, Colonel Montagu of the Blues, had made a discreet approach to the police through a third party trying to gauge the strength of the case against his young officer. Finally, Monro had added as a bitter afterthought the news that Hammond's escape to America had been a complete success.

On the following day, Thursday, October 10, an evidently exasperated Commissioner Monro fired off two more notes to the durable Cuffe. The first drew Cuffe's attention to the fact that Lord Arthur Somerset was still in Badminton — "I can only deplore the delay which is being made in high quarters about this horrible case." The second presented a further complication on the Arthur Newton front. Monro evidently felt that the DPP's office was dragging its heels on the issue of whether the solicitor should be prosecuted for attempting to abduct Algernon Allies. Newton's habit of writing letters to the DPP complaining about Inspector Abberline's "protection" of the star witness did not exactly help to ease the friction. Monro wrote to Cuffe: "Mr Newton's letters are simply bounce, and he may find this policy awkward yet. If he or his clients try force, they will find it be 'no remedy'!. If he tries any more of his objectionable letters, I suggest your referring him to the Police. We shall deal with him."

Monro was obviously spoiling for a fight, but seems to have been unaware of the potent rumor that Newton was prepared to drag the name of Prince Albert Victor into the affair. Monro's reaction was that of a man who saw the entire case slipping away. Now that Hammond was beyond his jurisdiction, he had little or no grounds for holding Allies under his "protection" as, according to the Lord Chancellor's opinion, Allies's uncorroborated evidence was of insufficient strength. Monro had already felt obliged to issue instructions that P.C. Hanks be recalled from Badminton. The moment when an arrest could have been easily effected had passed, and the whole police operation seemed to be back at square one. Cuffe naturally felt the full intensity of Scotland Yard's resentment, and even his strong nerves were beginning to fray under the intense cross-pressure from those below signaling "forward" and those above signaling "back." On Friday, October 11, Cuffe again wrote to Sir Augustus Stephenson, who was still on holiday in Lochinch, detailing the latest developments, and his tone contains the suggestion of a whine. Cuffe was evidently feeling more than a bit of self-pity at the impossibility of the situation and though his reserve remains intact there is the implication that it might be about time that Sir Augustus came back to his post. Cuffe wrote: "None of the bigwigs who are conducting this case are in town or accessible to one another which does not expedite matters. . . . If they had boldly said at first that they would not prosecute on grounds of policy and sent the papers to the War Office — whether it was the right course or not — it would have been intelligible — but to go on picking holes in the evidence . . . seems to me incapable of justification."

The idea of sending the papers on the case to the War Office struck a responsive chord with the Attorney General; it had long been considered a fall-back position if the issue of a warrant or summons was deemed inadvisable. Sir Richard Webster indicated to Cuffe that he would issue instructions along these lines on the following Monday. It seemed a neat, if somewhat craven, solution to everyone's problem as it would take the heat off the politicians and civil servants and saddle the army with the problem of assessment. The War Office seemed to have more options: it could either ignore the evidence or try the case as a military offense or, most likely, see to it that Lord Arthur Somerset's "resignation" took place in a way that deftly indicated that he would be unwelcome in Society. The wretched Cuffe was assured of a quiet weekend while the Attorney General composed a letter to the Lord Chancellor in Braemar suggesting the War Office tactic and soliciting his opinion on the move.

On Wednesday, October 16, Lord Halsbury gave his considered opinion of the proposed tactic in a telegram to Sir Richard Webster. It read: "LETTER ONLY RECEIVED LAST NIGHT. I SAY CERTAINLY NOT."

This astonishing decision seemed to indicate that there were perhaps far greater depths to the case than either Cuffe, in the DPP's office, or Monro, at the Metropolitan Police headquarters, could guess, though they must have obtained some glimmerings of a clue from two surprise encounters the same day. That morning Commissioner Monro was visited in his office by two distinguished members of the royal household staff, General Sir Dighton Probyn and Sir Francis Knollys. Both were courtiers of the old school.

Sir Dighton Probyn had early proved his loyalty to the concept of empire by wielding his sabre with such brilliance during the Indian Mutiny that he had been awarded the Victoria Cross, among numerous other decorations. However, Sir Dighton was rather more than a Victorian Audie Murphy. He also possessed a remarkable sense of discretion.

He had earlier proved his worth to his royal master when the Prince had unwittingly made a dubious acquaintance some twelve years before. He had become fascinated by a young man whom he had met on the French Riviera called Count Miecislas Jaraczewski. The Count was invited to England and became a habitué of Sandringham and Malborough House. Sir Philip Magnus, the Prince's biographer, describes the Count with tactful understatement as "young, mysterious, good looking and evidently well bred." The Marlborough House set promptly adapted his name to the more acceptable and pronounceable "Sherry and Whiskers."

The good-looking Count had a short and hilarious run in London before the consequences of his misdeeds began to catch up. On the brink of public exposure, he obligingly swallowed prussic acid. Sir Dighton Probyn arranged for the formal inquest to be waived and took possession of his private papers. The Count was probably a blackmailer, but nevertheless the Prince of Wales attended his funeral and sent his personal wreath of flowers to grace the coffin.

Sir Francis Knollys was an even more seasoned expert in royal matters personal. His family had served the crown for over two hundred years. His father, Sir William Knollys, had been treasurer and comptroller of the Prince of Wales household and since 1880 Sir Francis himself had been confidential secretary to the Prince. It was largely his tact, discretion, and ability as a fixer that had made the unpleasant business of the Mordaunt divorce just bearable. Knollys went on to refine his rare skills and by 1889 was close to mastery of the delicate art of keeping the potentially damaging consequences of the Prince's peccadilloes, sexual and otherwise, down to a bare minimum. The Cleveland Street affair was in some ways the ultimate test of his skill.

He had no previous experience in handling a homosexual scandal and from the outset was evidently somewhat unsure of the details. Knollys and Probyn explained to Commissioner Monro that they had been sent by the Prince of Wales himself to try to establish exactly what was going on in the Cleveland Street case. Monro promptly passed the buck. He could tell them nothing, he explained, as the case was out of his hands and being conducted by the Public Prosecutor's office. Shortly afterwards the same two emissaries called on Cuffe in the Treasury building.

A record of the meeting survives in Cuffe's scrawled note "for the record." Cuffe's handwriting, not very legible at the best of times, seemed to respond to stress by compression of the characters. The word formation in his note on the meeting is almost horizontal with barely controlled tension. Most of its looks like a series of dashes broken up by space, but some parts are just about decipherable: ". . . said P. of Wales was in a great state, didn't believe a word of it and wished he could come himself to clear LAS — and must have something settled. . . . They pressed strongly that an answer or decision should be come to . . . could tell them nothing without instructions. . . . I said I understood their feelings. . . ."

From these lines and reasonable conjecture about other somewhat less legible passages, it is possible to reconstruct the circumstances of the meeting. Cuffe is undoubtedly awed by such a deputation, yet his sense of concern for the royal family's private anxieties does not triumph over his awareness of public duty as a servant of the Crown. Cuffe does the correct thing and courteously refuses to pass on any public secrets on his own responsibility. He can disclose nothing about Lord Arthur Somerset or any other aspect of the case. The courtiers are advised to return on the following day, after he had obtained further advice. But if Cuffe's note is anything to go by, his state of nerves when confronted by the two members of the royal household must have been obvious, particularly to an experienced operator like Sir Francis Knollys. There could be little doubt that Lord Arthur Somerset was in grave trouble. There are times when a "no comment" is more instructive than any number of explanations, and this was undoubtedly one such occasion.

Sir Francis, having received a commitment for a further meeting, was not going to let Cuffe off the hook. He was a master at delicately keeping up the pressure. That same evening, he sent a message to Cuffe on Marlborough House notepaper: "Dear Cuffe, Probyn has returned to Sandringham [the Royal country house in Norfolk] but will be back for a night on Friday evening here early in the morning of that day. I will remain here until 7 o'clock this evening and could either meet you at Marlborough House or at the Treasury at any time you like to name tomorrow." Meanwhile, Cuffe was racing round London in a desperate quest for "instructions." Sir Richard Webster, the Attorney General, was as usual difficult to locate when there was a hard choice to be made. During most of the summer he had exercised his responsibility for the case at long-range, either from his home in Surrey or his parliamentary constituency in the Isle of Wight. As luck would have it, Cuffe learned that Sir Richard was again passing through town en route to the Isle of Wight. Cuffe hired a cab and managed to intercept the peripatetic Attorney General before he got on the train at London Bridge station. Cuffe received his "instructions" and noted them down on his return to the office. His handwriting was much improved. The Attorney General's instructions were that in the event of another meeting Cuffe was "to inform Sir D Probyn and Sir F Knollys, if possible verbally in the presence of others: 'That all papers in Veck and Newlove case had been before the AG [Attorney General] under whose directions I am acting in this case. That I have seen him [the Attorney General] since you called and that he is unable to authorise me to make any communication to you respecting the contents of these pp. No inference to be drawn from his refusal.' " Cuffe, in essence, was given the reassurance he needed. He was to tell the courtiers to mind their own business, albeit with a proper formality and deference. It is in some ways an impressive note — loyalty to the institution of the Crown was more important than loyalty to the person who might be king. That evening, Cuffe settled down to write yet another letter to Sir Augustus Stephenson and recounted the dramatic events of the day. There is a sense of muted outrage, triggered by the Lord Chancellor's persistent absences in Scotland and aggravated by the Attorney General's fondness for the Isle of Wight being indulged at times of crisis in the case. Again there appears to be an underlying hint that Sir Augustus himself, having recovered from the battering he received in the early battles, should return to the front. The war to preserve his department's integrity was still very much on. Cuffe's judgment of the next most probable development was contained in the line: "I expect he [the Prince of Wales] will now tell his people to go to the AG [Attorney General]."

Cuffe was a shrewd judge of a situation, but Knollys and Probyn were, it seems, much shrewder. The next day, October 17, came and went without any ostensible developments.

Cuffe, having nothing to add to the comments in his original interview, did not get in touch with Knollys. And Knollys, having precisely judged that Cuffe was not the kind of public servant who could be lured into unauthorized disclosure of official secrets, did not bother to take up the offer of a further interview. Cuffe had to come to him; if he did not, Knollys knew he had to go elsewhere. Cuffe's hour of greatness had come and gone. And he must have been extremely happy when Sir Augustus Stephenson returned to the office on the morning of Friday, October 18.

Though physically and mentally refreshed by his holiday, Sir Augustus was evidently in a state of considerable anxiety about the next move. His first action was to write to the Attorney General, reporting himself back and fit for duty and underlining the fact that he was fully in agreement with all that his assistant had done in his absence. But he also went on: "I have the honour to be personally known to HRH [His Royal Highness, the Prince of Wales] — my brother is one of his equerries — and it is in my judgement most probable

— that were HRH in England — some enquiries would be made of me — either directly or through my brother — confidentially — that would have me in a position of difficulty. . . . Of one thing I am certain — that HRH will not allow the matter to rest as it is."

Although the private documents on the case seem to convey an impression that the Prince was literally breathing down the necks of the bureaucracy, he was, in fact, far, far away. But the sound of heavy royal breathing, like the empire, could almost girdle the globe. At the end of September he left Scotland and joined the Princess of Wales in Denmark for a few days. He then proceeded to Venice for a fortnight's stay. On October 15, the day before Knollys's and Probyn's confrontation with Cuffe, the Prince embarked with the Princess and his two sons, Prince Eddy and Prince George, on the royal yacht *Osborne*, and set sail for Athens.

What Queen Victoria described as "the royal mob" was assembling in the Greek capital for the wedding of the Prince of Wales's nephew, Constantine, Duke of Sparta, and the German Emperor's sister, Princess Sophie. It was to be a happy family occasion and, incidentally, a useful demonstration of British imperial power that was unlikely to escape the notice of other crowned heads. As the *Osborne* ploughed through the Adriatic towards Athens, it was escorted by the entire British Mediterranean fleet.

For Prince Eddy, the member of the royal family most directly menaced by the Cleveland Street rumors, it was to be the start of a series of royal and imperial junkets that would keep him out of Britain for the next eight months. The Prince of Wales was by this stage of his career well used to operating at many levels. On the apparently serene royal surface the only ripple was the Prince's relationship with the

Kaiser, who attended a luncheon aboard the British flagship *Dreadnought* wearing the uniform of a British Admiral of the Fleet. The Prince of Wales nobly maintained his good humor while the Kaiser solemnly outlined his opinions of how the British fleet should make its continental dispositions.

Thus, as the Cleveland Street affair approached its climax, the Prince of Wales was establishing the most perfect of alibis for royal noninvolvement in the proper processes of justice. As far as the public was concerned, his role was totally above suspicion: he was not only out of the country but also on the high seas, deep in the most innocent family concerns.

On Friday, October 18, the various strands of royal involvement in the Cleveland Street affair finally came together. Sir Francis Knollys and Sir Dighton Probyn had decided to elevate the exercise of royal influence. It is clear now from the private papers, and must have been clear to the sophisticated Knollys at the time, that those with direct responsibility — ranging from Commissioner Monro to Attorney General Sir Richard Webster — might be dazzled by the spectacle of royal influence in action and display exaggerated courtesy. Yet they all appreciated the distinction between bending and breaking the rules.

Lord Arthur Somerset, having left Badminton two days earlier, was in London and had already given his servant orders to pack his more personal belongings in preparation for a possible journey abroad. That morning he met Sir Dighton Probyn by arrangement and strongly asserted that his name would be vindicated. Sir Dighton, however, did not, in the light of subsequent events, seem entirely reassured by the word of Lord Arthur as an officer and a gentleman. Nevertheless, they agreed to meet for dinner that evening at the Marlborough Club. That afternoon the Prime Minister,

Lord Salisbury, was returning from France, and on landing at Dover was handed a telegram from Sir Dighton Probyn requesting a meeting in London. Lord Salisbury replied with a telegram to say that he would be passing through town (on his way to the family home of Hatfield House, Hertfordshire) and offering to meet him at King's Cross Station before the departure of the seven o'clock train on the Great Northern Line. It was by any observable standards a casual occasion. The essence of the meeting was that Lord Salisbury, in response to Sir Dighton Probyn's question, said that Lord Arthur Somerset had by no means escaped the threat of arrest. This was all that Sir Dighton needed to know. The conversation was oblique but to the point, though it caused a modest delay in the Prime Minister's schedule. He missed the seven o'clock train home and had to catch the half-past seven instead.

One hour after this meeting Lord Arthur Somerset broke his appointment to dine with Sir Dighton Probyn at the Marlborough Club. Sir Dighton, it seems, had indicated at their morning meeting that he himself might be a little late for dinner — he planned a mid-evening engagement with the Prime Minister. There was finesse in the operation to the very last. Instead of spending a convivial evening with his friend, Lord Arthur took the velvety hint. He arranged for his luggage to be loaded into a cab and once more set off for Europe. By the next morning Lord Arthur Somerset was established, for the time being, at Vimille, near Boulogne.

Later in the year some details of this minuet of honor and corruption emerged publicly, but all those in public positions were able to protest their probity with great fervor. There was no question in the minds of the key participants that royal influence had been used to pervert the natural course of justice. On October 25, exactly a week after Lord

Arthur Somerset's hasty departure, the royal yacht *Osborne* docked at Piraeus. The Prince of Wales, learning the outcome of his earlier initiative, wrote a very civil letter to Lord Salisbury. He expressed satisfaction that Lord Arthur Somerset had been allowed to flee the country, and made one more request. HRH wished to ensure that should Lord Arthur "ever dare to show his face in England again," the Prime Minister would permit him to visit his parents quietly in the country "without fear of being apprehended on this awful charge."

From the royal point of view it may have seemed an elegant and successful operation. But there were other ways of looking at it which were equally valid. Understandably, perhaps, a section of the popular press was less enthralled by the spectacle of Lord Arthur Somerset being allowed to escape justice while men of lower social position were serving jail sentences for similar crimes. *The North London Press* subsequently printed a poem about the aristocrat's flight, which, despite its plebeian irreverence, grasped the fundamental point:

> *My Lord Gomorrah sat in his chair*
> *Sipping his costly wine;*
> *He was safe in France, that's called the fair;*
> *In a city some call 'Boo-line'*
> *He poked the blaze and he warmed his toes,*
> *And, as the sparks from the logs arose,*
> *He laid one finger beside his nose —*
> *And my Lord Gomorrah smiled.*
>
> *He thought of the wretched, vulgar tools*
> *Of his faederastian joys* [sic],
> *How they lay in prison, poor scapegoat fools;*

Raw, cash-corrupted boys.
While he and his "pals" the "office" got
From a "friend at Court", and were off like a shot,
Out of reach of Law, Justice, and "that — rot,"
And my Lord Gomorrah smiled.

SEVEN

A Royal Passage
to India

The abrupt departure of Lord Arthur Somerset had a twofold effect on the printout of the rumor machine. The "responsible" rumor had it that Lord Arthur was an innocent victim of the malevolence of the lower orders determined to drag the aristocracy into the mire. The "irresponsible" rumor had it that Lord Arthur was the sodomite-in-waiting to the royal family, the medium through which Prince Albert Victor was able to indulge his unnatural lusts.

It was the "responsible" rumor that most concerned the police. Throughout October Commissioner Monro had bombarded the DPP's office and the Home Office with "confidential" memoranda and letters requesting "instructions." On October 22, four days after Lord Arthur Somerset's flight, he rolled all his resentment into one ball and hurled it as yet another memorandum at the DPP. He began by referring to his letter of 25 September (outlining the Allies abduction incident) when he brought to the DPP's notice what seemed to amount to a conspiracy by certain persons to defeat the ends of justice. The police had since ascertained that one of the persons, Arthur Newton, was Lord Arthur Somerset's solicitor. Monro then came to the core of his complaint: "Inaction has been publicly attributed to the Metropolitan Police in connection with this case, and this assertion, absolutely groundless as it is, has now been magnified into an accusation against the Police of bringing an unfounded charge against the nobleman in question."

The Commissioner then logged the number of outstanding questions on which the police required answers. It made an impressive list:

I should be glad to be informed a) whether the charge against the nobleman in question with reference to which there is evidence in possession of yourself and the police is to be proceeded with b) if so, what action is to be taken by the police, either acting under your orders or of their own motion c) whether the charge against the Solicitors Clerk [Taylerson], and others is to be proceeded with either by yourself or, if not, whether the Police are at liberty to take such proceedings in the matter as they may be advised d) whether you desire the boy Allies as a witness for the Crown to be still secured against any attempt to remove him from this country, or the Metropolitan Police District.

On the following day, Sir Augustus Stephenson, now back in the DPP's office, replied bleakly: "Conduct of the prosecution undertaken by me by direction of the Secretary of State and since conducted under direction of the Attorney-General has been for some time past and now is entirely out of my hands. I am not in a position to give you any answer or any information on any of the matters on which you ask for information." Sir Augustus had clearly decided that wherever the buck might be, it was not to be found lying about in his office. Only a few days earlier he had responded to a Home Office inquiry about the case by saying: "The responsibility of the course hitherto adopted is not with me — and I am not called upon to express any opinion on the state of affairs as they are now."

The heat was now focused entirely on Sir Richard Webster, the Attorney General, who, as had happened once before when Lord Arthur Somerset was known to be out of the country, began to feel his indignation at the offense rising. Early in November, Sir Richard finally told the Lord Chancellor that he was not taking any more advice. He would act — as the law required — on his own responsibility. On Monday, November 4, the DPP had occasion to contact Sir Richard about the type of reply that should be sent to the solicitor Arthur Newton, who was again pressing for an interview with Algernon Allies, the chief material witness against Lord Arthur Somerset. Sir Richard replied in a friendly fashion saying that Sir Augustus could come round for a conference at any time but the reply to Newton could not be sent until the following Monday. Sir Augustus's response on the next day was icily polite: "As the answer to Mr Newton cannot be given until after Monday next — I infer from what I read in the newspapers that a decision as to the course to be taken will be come to on Friday — and as nothing which we in this department can say will influence that decision — there can be no object in our troubling you to give us a hearing on the subject. I presume you are aware of the fact that there are rumours implicating several persons *besides* those whose names have been mentioned in the statements that have been before us and you."

Two days later Sir Richard authorized application to be

made for an arrest warrant against Lord Arthur Somerset. The warrant was issued at Marlborough Street police court on November 12 based on informations sworn by Allies, the two post office boys Thickbroom and Swinscow, and Allies's mother, Elizabeth, who confirmed Lord Arthur's generosity to her son. The other deponents were the policemen Abberline, Hanks, and Sladden. There was no official comment on the remarkable fact that statements of all these people had been in the possession of the authorities for at least ten weeks, in most cases much longer. The formal charge was that Lord Arthur Somerset had committed "divers acts of gross indecency" with Allies and Thickbroom at 19 Cleveland Street between October 1887 and 5 July 1889.

It was some time before the press learned that a warrant had in fact been issued, but several alert newspapermen noticed the entry in the November 9 issue of the *Gazette* reporting that Lord Arthur Somerset's resignation from the Guards had been accepted. There was nothing in the bald facts of the report to suggest any sinister circumstance about Lord Arthur's resignation. If an army officer were not considered worthy of honorable discharge, it was inserted in the *Gazette* that his services were dispensed with. But the popular press was now ready to put constructions on the most innocent-seeming references to Lord Arthur Somerset. *The Birmingham Post* was the first to speculate. "It is impos-were in tune with the Regency; so was his reckless gambling. mentionable scandal, "until the police authorities take action against those who are alleged to be the chief offenders to indicate plainly in print names which are on every lip in all the clubs of the Metropolis; but since the issue within the past few days of certain official announcements, these are being mentioned on the street corners as well. . . ."

On November 14, the redoubtable Henry Labouchere made his first intervention in the affair through the columns of his magazine *Truth*. His information was a shade out of date as he was evidently unaware that a warrant for Lord Arthur Somerset's arrest had been issued. But he was obviously well acquainted with the struggle that had gone on in the bureaucracy of law enforcement. In what was to prove the first of many articles on the subject in *Truth*, Labouchere wrote:

The facts are in the hands of the Home Office and of Scotland-Yard, but as some of the greatest hereditary names of the country are mixed up in the scandal, every effort is being made to secure the immunity of the criminals. Indeed, I am credibly informed that the Home Office is throwing obstacles in the way of prompt action on the part of Scotland Yard, and trying to get the persons concerned out of the country before warrants are issued.

Very possibly our Government of the classes is of the opinion that the revelations which would ensue, were the criminals put on trial, would deal a blow to the reign of the classes, and to the social influence of the aristocracy. Let them, however, understand that they will not be allowed to protect their friends. It would be really too monstrous if crimes which, when committed by poor ignorant men, lead to sentences of penal servitude, were to be done with impunity by those whom the Tory Government delights to honour. The names are known. I warn Mr Matthews [the Home Secretary] that if he does not take action in this matter, there will be a heavy reckoning when Parliament meets. It is full time that the severest examples should bring home to all that there are certain foul crimes (too prevalent of late, by all accounts) that we cannot tolerate amongst us, unless London is to be regarded as the disgrace and opprobrium of modern civilisation.

The tone was typical Labouchere, raising the specific events from the level of a peephole scandal to one involving great issues of class, bureaucratic competence, and equality before the law. Few men have been more unfairly treated by history than Labouchere. Libertarians of the present day tend to recall him only as the author of the "Labouchere Amendment" and mark him down as some kind of unreconstructed Victorian queer-basher. While it is true that Labouchere, like most of his contemporaries, had a highly developed aversion to homosexuality (for which the modern psychologist might find some sinister explanation), his motives in introducing the amendment sprang in large measure from his concern for equality before the law. Armed with W. T. Stead's dossier on the increase in homosexual houses in the West End, Labouchere thought it ridiculous that the Act of 1885 should penalize forms of heterosexual exploitation without making adjustments in the homosexual sphere. Yet the amendment, which ironically has become his historical motif, was only one of innumerable issues Labouchere raised and fought over and, on most of them, a modern radical would be compelled to agree that Labouchere was right years, sometimes decades, ahead of his time. In fact, there has never since been anyone quite like Labouchere in British public life.

Henry Du Pre Labouchere was born on 9 November 1831 at 16 Portland Square, London, in what a contemporary described with some delicacy as circumstances that placed him beyond the need of money. Throughout a long life that started in the reign of William IV, spanned the Victorian and Edwardian eras, and ended in the reign of George V, Labouchere was a great source of anecdotes. But it is hard to find one, from the earliest to the last, that sounds characteristically Victorian. His devil-may-care attitude and hauteur were in tune with the Regency; so was his reckless gambling. His shabbiness was a whim of his own, his republicanism something he had picked up in America, his radicalism genuinely democratic in sentiment.

The facts of his wealth, his Huguenot ancestry, and above all his kaleidoscopic personality combined to make him probably the only man in England who was in the aristocratic Establishment without being of it and who could thus say, think, and do precisely what he fancied. His complete lack of deference for the Prince of Wales personified his stance vis-à-vis Victorian society as a whole. And although the Prince often found it refreshing, their relationship was naturally not untroubled. For "Labby," as he was universally known, was combative by instinct, and chose in an age of conformity to elevate an ingrained taste for the outrageous into an art form. Labby's wealth enabled him to be genuinely disinterested, quite apart from his temperamental readiness to become involved as soon as he scented an injustice.

The money stemmed from his grandfather, Pierre-César, a Huguenot from one of the numerous families that had settled in Belgium and Holland as havens from religious strife where they might give themselves over to the worship of their rigorous God and the diligent pursuit of commercial wealth. Pierre-César made the breakthrough. He was employed as an ill-paid but obviously gifted clerk in a trading company and bank, the House of John Hope, which had its headquarters in Amsterdam. He came to London on their behalf in 1792 and while doing business with the already eminent bank of Baring's decided he wanted to marry Dorothy Baring, the third daughter of the bank's owner, Sir Francis. When asked for his daughter's hand, the banker said no. When the young clerk asked if the information that he was shortly to become a partner in the prestigious House of Hope gave Sir Francis second thoughts, the banker unhesitatingly admitted this to be so. Apparently he was already far-sighted enough to be thinking in terms of a dynasty and so was John Hope when Pierre-César used an identical technique on him. At first he refused the demanded partnership; but the moment he heard that his clerk had become engaged to Dorothy Baring (which, strictly speaking, was by no means the case) he too changed his mind.

Using his wits and his family connections, Pierre-César Labouchere made an immense fortune. After the Napoleonic wars his bank underwrote the entire French government by floating the so-called Alliance Loan from which they collected 9 percent. His two sons, Labby's father and uncle, continued the tradition of amassing wealth. Labby inherited large fortunes from them both; his uncle, Lord Taunton, had engaged in profitable American ventures for several years before returning home, going into public life, and defeating Disraeli, the future Tory Prime Minister, at an election in the West Country constituency from which he took his title. Labby's father was more retiring but just as rich, and when he handed it over to his son after thirty years of impeccable direction, the bank was a power in London, which meant the commercial and financial markets of the world. With this kind of security behind him, Labby presented himself at Trinity College, Cambridge in 1850 and devoted himself to pleasure, a pursuit which continued unabated during his various careers as an adventurer, stock exchange speculator, diplomat, journalist, and politician. Labby's inglorious spell as an undergraduate earned him national notoriety before he was twenty-one. In the course of what was at best spasmodic attendance at the ancient university he ran up debts to the Newmarket bookmakers which amounted to a truly staggering £6,000. As a young man about London he frequented the leading bohemian establishment of the period, The Caves of Harmony off the Strand, described by Thackeray in *The Newcomes*. He was an energetic heterosexual and an enthusiastic fan of the girls who frequented the Caves — a contemporary describes the place as "equally devoted to the pursuits of Bacchus and Venus." Paddy Green, headwaiter there, said of the young Labby's escapades, "Mr. Leeboocheer was his own worst enemy."

In his early twenties Labby went to America and found an emotional home. In California he searched for gold he did not need. In New England he once spent two nights on a bench on Boston Common, temporarily out of funds after receiving lessons in a newly evolved card game called poker. All this by way of preparation for a career in Her Majesty's Diplomatic Service, which included one memorably undiplomatic card game with the Turkish ambassador to the Czarist court of St. Petersburg. Faced with the loss of the equivalent of $20,000 on one hand, Labby had quick-wittedly saved the day by "accidentally" playing a trump card out of turn, thus invalidating the hand. Reproached later for sharp practice, he was unabashed: "It is the essence of the game of whist to take every advantage," he said.

He was offered the post of British consul in Buenos Aires, which could in itself be construed as a mark of the Foreign Secretary's displeasure. Labby was unabashed and sent an airy acceptance — on condition that he could "discharge his consular duties" from Baden-Baden, a spa noted as much for its casino as for its health cure. Miraculously, he somehow contrived to stay in the diplomatic service for ten years, but his temperament demanded a wider canvas. By the middle 1860s he found it as a journalist and politician, winning and losing two constituencies in the space of five years. Writing was to supply his taste for adventure and controversy during the periods — and they were considerable — when he could not find a constituency. He was to be beseiged inside Paris during the Commune of 1870, sending stories to *The Daily News*, of which he owned a majority share, by a balloon called *Celeste*. The balloon was eventually shot down by the Prussians, but Labby kept on rising. In 1877 he started *Truth*, a magazine that rapidly established itself as an enemy of all forms of corruption, and three years later he finally achieved a secure Parliamentary base as the Radical member for Northampton. Labby in the House and *Truth* outside it were anti-Tory, anti-Establishment, anti-Sabbatarian, anti-teetotal (though Labby, surprisingly, was abstemious himself after being nauseated as a boy at Eton after an experiment with punch), anti-Imperialist, anti-cant, and anti-Royalist.

> *[With] Grandchildren not a few*
> *Great grandchildren too —*
> *She has been blest.*
> *We've been their sureties,*
> *Paid them gratuities,*
> *Pensions, annuities,*
> *God Save the Queen.*

This was a cheerful parody of the British national anthem that Labby had jotted on the back of a program while attending a first night at the theater, ironically named the Royalty, which his wife Henrietta Hodson, a former actress, launched and made brilliantly successful in the 1860s.

Her Majesty was not amused; nor was the Prince of Wales, with whom Labby shared many tastes — notably chorus girls and high-stake gambling and Clubland gossip. Above all, the Prince and Labby shared a habit of insolence and a deeply ingrained antipathy toward the acceptance of any restraints.

"Do you want me to drown my children like puppy dogs?" inquired the incensed heir to the throne of the greatest empire the world had ever seen when he next met the radical M.P.

"No, sir" Labby replied. "I simply believe that you should live within your income." The Prince was enraged by such bourgeois sentiments in the mouth of a man who had made extravagance a way of life.

Labby's attacks on the royal family and their expenditure continued for two decades and were of great relevance to the stance he adopted over the Cleveland Street affair. For Queen Victoria he was "that horrible lying Labouchere," apropos of some particularly hurtful remarks about her incompetent military son, the Duke of Cambridge. "No more uplifting patriotic spectacle can be imagined," Labby had written, "than the Duke standing at the head of his troops, his drawn salary in his hand." The attempt to expose Lord Arthur Somerset for his homosexual adventures in Hammond's brothel brought royal mother and son into unexpected and rare agreement. For three years, after which they were reconciled in France through the intercession of an equerry, the Prince of Wales referred to his tormentor as "that viper Labouchere."

Certainly no one else of Labouchere's class could have poked his nose into the Cleveland Street affair (referred to delicately as "the West End scandals"), decided that the Establishment had mounted a camouflage operation, and denounced it without fear of the consequences.

Emboldened by the support of Labouchere for its campaign, Ernest Parke's *North London Press* decided to take a major risk. Its coverage of the "hideous and foetid gangrene" had been unexciting for some weeks. The campaign needed a new impetus. On November 16, under the headline, "The West-End Scandals: Names of some of the Distinguished Criminals who have Escaped," *The North London Press* recalled the paper's original "scoop" and its willingness to name the aristocrats involved in the "indescribably loathsome scandal." It then reported:

> The men to whom we thus referred were
> THE EARL OF EUSTON,
> eldest son of the Duke of Grafton, and
> LORD H. ARTHUR C. SOMERSET,
> a younger son of the Duke of Beaufort.
> The former, we believe, has departed for Peru; the latter, having resigned his commission and his office of Assistant Equerry to the Prince of Wales, has gone too. These men have been allowed to leave the country and thus defeat the ends of justice because their prosecution would disclose the fact that a far more distinguished and more highly placed personage than themselves was inculpated in their disgusting crimes. The criminals in this case are to be numbered by the score. They include two or three members of Parliament, one of them being a popular Liberal.

Unfortunately for the credibility of Ernest Parke and *The North London Press*, the Earl of Euston was not in Peru. He was in 4 Grosvenor Place, London. On hearing that his name had been publicly mentioned in connection with the Cleveland Street scandal, Lord Euston instructed his solicitor to institute proceedings against Parke for criminal libel. On Saturday, November 30, Justice Field granted his fiat for the commencement of proceedings against Parke and on the afternoon of the same day a warrant for the editor's arrest was issued by the Bow Street police court. When Parke learned that a warrant had been issued, he went at once to Bow Street, accompanied by a friend who offered bail of £1,500. But by the time of their arrival the magistrate had left and Parke was kept in the cells until the following Monday, when he was allowed out on two sureties of £50 each. After a brief committal hearing, Parke was directed to stand trial at the next session of the Central Criminal Court.

The press was outraged at the thought of a fellow journalist languishing in the cells when there was no suggestion of his fleeing justice — quite the reverse. Although none cared to reprint the allegation against Lord Euston (or even Lord Arthur Somerset), they were united in their condemnation of the procedure adopted by the authorities. While awaiting trial, Parke became something of a popular hero among London's radical working class. At a mass meeting of Radical clubs in North London, a Mr. T. Tongue, president of the Borough of Hackney club, called for a public inquiry and proposed a vote of thanks for Parke's services to the community by exposing "the horrible doings which had taken place in the West End." A Mr. J. Knifton, one of the Shoreditch club, strongly supported the motion. Working men, he maintained, had a right to have an explanation: "Bringing up our boys as we have to do, we should not submit to a state of things which might end in their temptation, for their tempters are men of position and wealth. Working men are free from the taint, and for gold laid down our boys might be tempted to their fall."

An appeal was launched for Parke, the Fair Trial Fund to help defray the expenses of the impending libel action. It was organized by a young journalist on *The Star*, H. W. Massingham, who later became one of the most famous newspapermen of his time. One of the most generous donors was T. P. O'Connor, the Irish Nationalist and M.P. for Liverpool, who contributed £86. "Lover of Pluck and Fair Play" donated £6,6s; S. M. Burroughs (of Burroughs and Wellcome) contributed £2; and the list of minor contributors contained a sprinkling of justices of the peace and Members of Parliament as well as the cartmen and members of the Publishing and Machine Room of *The Star*. The weirdest *nom de plume* (used by a ten-shilling contributor) was "Ye see yon birkie ca'd a lord" ("birkie" was a Scottish slang term for a swaggering fellow).

On a less parochial scale, the immediate effect of the Parke action was to attract the interest of the foreign press which had been gently probing the scandal for some time without being able to find a suitable handhold. Now that some of the names were, in a sense, public, the American and continental publications plunged in with relish, uninhibited by the English libel laws. *La Lanterne* in Paris soon had *une douzaine de Lords* mixed up in the scandal. French readers, already gorged on stories about London's most famous murderer, *Jacques L'Evrentreur* (Jack the Stomach Opener), welcomed the change of diet. This was an altogether better class of *affaire*. In New York a portrait of Prince Albert Victor was used to illustrate an article about the West End scandals. The "irresponsible" rumor was finally getting its public airing. Various deductions were made about why Prince Eddy had undertaken a long Royal Tour of India as the Cleveland Street affair began to surface in public print.

The obvious damage to the monarchy by such stories was beginning to worry the Tories in Parliament. This was becoming more than a radical romp to embarrass the ruling class. Louis Jennings, the Conservative M.P. for Stockport, became almost as ardent in his private demands for an investigation as Labouchere himself, if only to clear the air. On November 23, Jennings, writing as "A Member of Parliament" to *The New York Herald,* tried to deflect the tide of rumor from the royal household: "Conjecture runs wild and scarcely anyone is spared. For this reason, among others, and guided by his usual discretion and knowledge of the world, The Prince of Wales, immediately on his return to London this week threw the whole weight of his influence against any further attempts at concealment."

The Prince of Wales had not been idle since he had privately congratulated Lord Salisbury on allowing Lord Arthur Somerset to leave the country (and incidentally escape British justice). After the "royal mob" wedding in Athens on October 27 he had taken the *Osborne* to Egypt with Prince Eddy in tow. They were met at Port Said by Sir Evelyn Baring, whose prosaic title of British Agent and Consul-General failed to conceal from the Egyptians the fact that he was the ruler of their country. He struck the Prince of Wales as "a very able man but with no manners." Prince Eddy soon made off for his grand tour of India while his father stayed on to do the ceremonial honors for the benefit of the empire in the Middle East. His official host, the Khedive Twefik — described by the Prince of Wales as "quite charming and full of conversation" — put the exquisite Ghizeh Palace in Cairo at his disposal. On November 2, the Prince repaid the hospitality at a great military review by leading 1,700 men of the British occupation force and 4,000 Egyptians in march past the Khedive. The massed British regimental bands played the Khedival Hymn and "God Save the Queen." On November 4, he attended a Mohammedan religious festival to honor the Prophet's birthday.

On leaving the country, the Prince in high good humor told Baring that he hoped the British would stay in Egypt forever. He then set off for home, stopping en route in Athens and Paris. The Paris stop, which seemed designed to improve the Prince's personal finances, caused the British ambassador, Lord Lytton, some headaches. On November 14, Lytton confidentially informed Lord Salisbury that he had found it necessary to make private inquiries through the head of the French police "with a view to the protection of H.R.H." from "the abuse of his name and position" by shady financiers. On November 18, the Prince arrived back in Marlborough House and promptly set about the task of dousing rumors about his son's involvement in the Cleveland Street scandal. He was not entirely successful.

On Friday, December 6, the Post Office formally discharged the boys who had given evidence about the goings-on in Cleveland Street; they had been under suspension with pay for almost five months. Deprived of their modest source of unearned income, they were obliged to try and find another "position." After so long a period under police surveillance it was only natural that the more practical among them should ask someone on the force for advice. Thickbroom and Perkins in particular had established a close relationship with the dogged stakeout man P.C. Sladden. For some weeks after the trial of Veck and Newlove they accompanied Sladden every evening on watch outside St. James's Club. Inspector Abberline had instructed them to point out any other "gentlemen" whom they recognized as Cleveland Street customers. The vigil had proved abortive in terms of identification evidence, but Sladden seemed to develop a paternal concern for the boys' welfare. The boys called him "Jack."

On the day of their suspension, Thickbroom and Perkins called at Scotland Yard to see, first, whether Inspector Abberline could do anything for them. They met P.C. Luke Hanks who said that Abberline was busy and could not meet them until the following week; Hanks was sorry to hear about their dismissal but had no practical suggestions. As Abberline had never been "too busy" to see them before, the boys decided to take their troubles to "Jack." That evening they went round to P.C. Sladden's house to see if he could think of anything that might help. As it happened, Sladden could, though only in the most guarded terms. He suggested that there might be a possible benefactor who would take pity on their situation. "I know somebody," said Sladden, "who wants to know when you are dismissed and who asked me to tell him. I'll go and do so and let you know." The boys understood that the "somebody" was Lord Arthur Somerset's father.

The impression grew stronger on the following day when, as arranged, they met Sladden on his beat in the Tottenham Court Road. Sladden's fellow beat-basher, a P.C. Walker, told them "You leave it in the hands of the toffs and you will be all right. I know myself there will be a thousand pounds down." Sladden and his friend were clearly ready to ease their own and everyone else's lot with some highly irregular "fixing."

Following Sladden's instructions, Thickbroom and Perkins kept an appointment with their potential benefactor at 2 P.M. on the following Monday at the corner of Oxford Street and Poland Street in the West End. They were not met by Lord Arthur Somerset's father but by the ubiquitous solicitor Arthur Newton, who had a proposition. The outlines of it were that if they could round up all the boys involved in the case they could start a new life in Australia on handsome terms. They would have £50 down, a new outfit, and £1 a week each for three years. Two or three other boys, he said, had gone away already and they were doing well. The whereabouts of Algernon Allies was mentioned and the boys thought he was still under police protection. Newton told them that Allies had been "a damned fool" and went on to ask whether they could get the other boys — Wright and

Swinscow and Veck's "private secretary," Barber — acquainted with the offer and bring them back to the same meeting place tomorrow. They undertook to try.

Perkins, Swinscow, and Wright turned up. Thickbroom sent his excuses — his father was ill. Barber could not be located. On this occasion they were met by De Gallo, Newton's inquiry agent, and taken to the private parlor of a nearby public house. They were, said De Gallo, to start that very night for Dover, in order to proceed to Calais and then Marseilles before finally taking ship to Australia. They would see somebody whom they knew on board the boat. One of them asked if it would be Mr. Newton. "Never mind," said De Gallo, "you'll know when you see him."

De Gallo later told them that the boat was full. He then took them to a coffeehouse in the Edgeware Road, gave them a sovereign for refreshments, and booked beds for them for that night. They were to wait in case Thickbroom should arrive. He also offered to deliver any tender farewell letters they might want to send to their parents. Swinscow and Perkins availed themselves of the offer.

The next day, when Mrs. Swinscow received the abrupt intelligence that her son was off to Australia, she hurried round to her local police station and demanded to know what was going on. The enterprise petered out feebly. Thickbroom never showed up and De Gallo, clearly losing enthusiasm for the project, decided to wind it up. At four o'clock on Wednesday afternoon he told the boys to forget about it and go home.

Unfortunately for De Gallo and his sponsors, the boys decided to go back to Inspector Abberline and tell him the whole story. Abberline told Commissioner Monro and they decided to make an example of Newton who they now saw as being involved in a pattern of malpractice dating back to the attempt to abduct Allies. On December 16, the Bow Street magistrate issued summonses against Newton, Taylerson, and De Gallo, charging them as follows:

On the 25th September, and at divers times between that and the 12th day of December, 1889, — did unlawfully conspire, combine, confederate, and agree together and with divers other persons to obstruct, pervert, and defeat the due course of law and justice in certain proceedings then pending at the Marlborough Police Court and in the Central Criminal Court in respect of offences alleged to have been committed by divers persons at 19, Cleveland Street, Fitzroy-square, in the County of London, and to obstruct, prevent, and defeat the due course of law and justice in respect to the said offence.

The summonses were issued with the full consent and backing of the DPP's office but not with full knowledge of all the facts. Out of loyalty to a colleague involved in a long, trying case, Abberline did not tell the DPP of P.C. Sladden's apparent defection to the other side. It was a detail, but a significant one. For it meant that even the police, the public authority which had held out longest against the subtle corruption of the whole affair, now had something to hide.

After its fright at the near loss of so many material witnesses, Scotland Yard tightened the security of its watch over Algernon Allies. He was moved from the Rose Coffee House in Hounsditch, and his new lodging was kept secret both from Arthur Newton and his own parents in Sudbury. In mid-December, the Treasury Solicitor received a plaintively respectful letter from Algernon's brother William. "Sir," wrote William, "Pardon the liberty I take in addressing these few lines to you, trusting at the same time it is not troubling you, but my Father asked me to write asking if you could kindly inform him of the whereabouts of my brother, as he is very anxious about him, for the weather is so very cold and

[137]

we want to send him some clothes and we know he must be in want of some now, and if you would kindly let me know we should be greatly obliged. Trusting to remain, Sir, Yours obediently." Sir Augustus Stephenson wrote back to say that he would be happy to forward anything he might send to Algernon, but his actual whereabouts remained an official secret as far as his own family was concerned. Allies spent the Christmas of 1889, as he had so many of the preceding months, under the oppressively benevolent eye of Inspector Abberline.

Another actor in the drama who spent that Christmas far from the bosom of his family was Prince Albert Victor, the Heir Presumptive. His absence at least gave those like Louis Jennings, the Tory M.P., who were busy trying to kill the rumors about the Prince, the chance to do their work with greater freedom. On December 22, Jennings, apparently with the connivance of the Prince of Wales, again wrote to *The New York Herald* as "A Member of Parliament." The tone of his letter, printed prominently on the editorial page, was severe: "Over and over again it has been whispered about that Prince Eddy would shortly be recalled from India under circumstances peculiarly painful to himself and his family. . . . It was impossible either to trace these reports to source or to check them. It may, however, put some slight restraint upon the gossip-mongers to be informed in a semi-official manner that the arrangements in connection with the young Prince's visit to India will not be altered in any way, and that he will return at the time originally fixed, and not before." Jennings felt that the whole matter had got out of hand because the proper law officers had not been allowed to do their duty. "Every day the name of some well-known man, who is perfectly free from blame, is added to the black-list which cowardly defamers circulate in private. Nobody is safe."

The word on Lord Arthur Somerset in December was that he had moved on from Boulogne, first to Brussels and then to Constantinople where he had offered his services to the Sultan as a military advisor. In Constantinople he had, according to Labouchere's magazine, *Truth,* explained that he had left England to "screen a highly-placed person." The Sultan apparently had no particular opening for Lord Arthur at that time and the runaway aristocrat had moved on to Hungary.

Prince Eddy himself was riding out the gossip-mongers at a hectic pace. After his fond farewell to his father at Port Said at the end of October, he finally arrived in India on November 6 and began a grueling imperial round under the protective eye of Sir Edward Bradford, V.C., later Chief Commissioner of the Metropolitan Police. The Prince was spared few of the subcontinent's attractions, though there was plenty of shooting and polo to break up the routine of scenic and historic wonders. He inspected the prison in which British soldiers had been imprisoned by Tippoo Sahib, visited the Residency in Lucknow, the memorial at Kanpur, Akbar's Fort, the Moti Musjid, and the Taj Mahal, and took his ease as the honored guest of the fabulously wealthy Nizam of Hyderabad. At Tennevelly he toured the Christian school and for light relief in the evening was entertained by a troupe of jugglers and Nautch dancing girls. After a stormy crossing of the Bay of Bengal, his party arrived in Rangoon shortly before Christmas. On Christmas Day Prince Eddy and his entourage attended divine service in the palace of the former King Theebaw, who had vacated the premises after being booted off his throne by the British five years earlier. On Boxing Day, the official chronicle of the tour recorded: "There was snipe-shooting in the morning (twenty-six couple), a garden party, at which the entertainment consisted of boat-races and tugs-of-war by men and women, and a dinner party." And so it went on, and on. The Khyber Pass, Peshawar, Rawalpindi, Lahore, Chunga Minga, Kapurthala, Amritsar, Delhi where "the Prince and one other gun went snipe-shooting bagging forty snipe, then a brace of partridges, and about ten head of miscellaneous game."

Back in the Mother Country, the growing number of interested spectators of the Cleveland Street affair had their attention drawn by a different type of entertainment. As the scandal accelerated into the New Year some kind of denouement seemed imminent.

Lord Euston's prosecution of the editor Ernest Parke was, after several postponements, firmly established for hearing in the January session at the Old Bailey. It was not the fate of Parke that excited public interest so much as the consequences for Lord Euston if his action failed, which would be tantamount to giving legal sanction to the allegations against him. Lord Euston had popularly been considered one of the most conspicuous heterosexuals of the epoch. Educated at Harrow and commissioned in the Rifle Brigade, he had established an early reputation as a "stage-door Johnny." At the age of twenty-three he married Kate Cook, the Variety Theatre actress. The marriage was not a great success and the couple separated after seven years. In 1884 they featured in exceptionally well-publicized divorce proceedings in which it emerged that Lady Euston had previously gone through a form of marriage with a commercial traveler called Mr. Smith. The Earl was considered somewhat lucky to escape proceedings for bigamy, but fortunately for him it was also discovered that the Mr. Smith in question had a wife living at the time of his "marriage" to Kate Cook, so that she was technically "free" when she married the Earl. After the divorce Lord Euston continued his interest in the theater but devoted more of his time to Freemasonry. When the Cleveland Street scandal broke he was Provincial Grand Master of Northamptonshire and Huntingtonshire.

According to Frank Harris, then editor of *The Fortnightly Review* and, if his autobiography *My Life and Loves* is to be believed, one of the great sexual athletes of all time, Lord Euston was "the last man in the world to be suspected of abnormal propensities." If the Parke trial established that such a man was a covert homosexual, there seemed no end to the potential for further revelations about sexual corruption in high places.

·➤❴ EIGHT ❵◆·

The Tenant of
"a Man Called Violet"

The trial of Ernest Parke, editor of *The North London Press*, opened at the Old Bailey on the morning of January 15, 1890. It was a classic set-piece Victorian trial, a self-conscious exhibition of justice in action, featuring the greatest legal talent of the day, and it drew a packed house. A reporter on *The Star* described how "the eyes of a court crowded to every corner were turned towards the raised enclosure of the dock. Mr Parke, with his clear-cut intellectual face and his waving auburn hair, standing out against the light from the window beyond, leisurely took off his coat and leaned over the front of the dock prepared to face the serious issue before him. Justice Hawkins, with his hard face, had taken his place on the bench."

Justice Hawkins, because of his nickname "Hanging

Hawkins," was one of the best-known judges of the period, though less famous than the leading counsel on the prosecution side, Sir Charles Russell, Q.C., who was later to become Lord Chief Justice. His junior was Mr. Charles Matthews, who later became Director of Public Prosecutions. The two defense counsel were Mr. Frank Lockwood, later Sir Frank, Solicitor General, and Mr. Herbert Asquith, afterwards Liberal Prime Minister. Parke repeated his earlier plea of "Not Guilty."

Sir Charles Russell opened the case by describing the libel as "one of a very serious character, but not wholly directed against Lord Euston" (an oblique reference to Lord Arthur Somerset). The libel was the more serious because Parke had pleaded "Not Guilty" but had added a plea of justification which implied that the libel itself was true. Lord Euston did not intend to take advantage of any technical objections to this form of plea, but would "meet the libel openly and wholly."

The house at 19 Cleveland Street, said Sir Charles, was now notorious; it had been used "for purposes of the most nefarious kind." He then read out the libel to the jury, and told the story of Lord Euston's one visit to the premises with the object of seeing *poses plastiques* (the Victorian equivalent of striptease).

The peer's "prurient curiosity," as Sir Charles put it, "did him no credit." But "directly the loathsome overtures made to him he threatened to knock down the man who made them unless he was at once allowed to leave the house." The policy of enticing people to the house may have been for what the French called *chartage* — *i.e.*, blackmailing those "who have been weak enough to resort to that place." In any event, Lord Euston had left and had never been back — the incident had taken place "one night in May or June last" and

[143]

that was the beginning and the end of Euston's connection with the place.

Euston's story of how he came to be there in the first place was thus first told by his counsel, although later when Russell called him to give evidence, Euston gave his own explanation in more detail: "I recollect being in Piccadilly last May or June, at about eleven at night, and having handed to me a card bearing the words — 'C. Hammond, 19 Cleveland Street, *Poses Plastiques*'. I put the card in my pocket and read it when I got home. About a week afterwards I drove up in a hansom to this place. As a matter of fact I have no private carriage. I occasionally use my father's. I went alone and got there about eleven. I rang the bell and the door was opened by a man of medium height, clean shaven except for a dark moustache, and with hair that was getting thin on the top [a fair description of Charles Hammond]. He took me into the first room on the right of the passage. He asked me for a sovereign, which I gave him, and then I asked him where these *poses plastiques* were going to take place. He said 'There's nothing of that sort here', and then stated the real character of the house. I asked him what he meant by saying such a thing as that to me, and told him that if he did not let me out I should knock him down. He opened the door and let me out, and I went away. At that time I did not mention the occurrence to anyone; but later on I mentioned the incident to some friends of mine."

Later in the year, as Sir Charles explained in his opening speech, Euston had heard his name mentioned in connection with the house and immediately did "what any honourable and honest man would have done" — consulted a solicitor and brought the charge against Parke. *The North London Press* libel had coupled his name with that of Lord Arthur Somerset, and had implied that Euston had left the country for Peru in order to escape a warrant that had either been issued against him or was in the offing. Russell knew that he was on a sure thing here and made great play with the question of "Peru," where Parke or his reporter had evidently slipped up. Russell said he was curious to see what evidence the defendants had in their possession at the time when "these scandalous statements" had been made. Lord Euston had in 1882 gone to Biarritz to visit a sick relative but, this humanitarian journey to foreign parts aside, he had not left England for years.

The justification plea — that the story Parke had printed was true — stated that Euston had visited Cleveland Street in May 1887 where he had committed indecent acts with John Saul, and went on to specify other occasions when Euston had gone there — for the same reason — with a Frank Hewett. Sir Charles said that Euston had heard these names *for the first time* when they appeared on the justification plea.

Russell then revealed the technique he had devised for pacing the case. He would begin by proving publication of the libel, call on the defense to justify it, and then put his own witness in the box — unless the judge ruled otherwise. If Euston appeared before the defense, he could do no more than make a general denial. If he came last, as Russell wanted, he could deal with the false assertions specifically. (He omitted to add that this unusual procedure gave the prosecution the important psychological advantage of having the last word with the jury.)

Mr. Justice Hawkins, "with his hard face," declined to express any opinion at all, which gave Russell what he wanted. After the technical matter of proving publication had been dealt with (*The North London Press*, it emerged, had printed a modest run of 4,500 copies), Lockwood was left to do the best he could with the defense case.

[145]

He opened with a spirited attack on Russell, who had described his client as being anxious to meet the charge, but was now, nonetheless, going to avoid preliminary cross-examination. Lockwood said that in his experience he had never known a case in which a man whose character had been attacked had deliberately shrunk from offering himself for such examination. Euston preferred to rely on the art and skill of his counsel — to weaken the evidence of the defense and then, "feeling his courage revived" sufficiently, to go into the box. Lockwood went on to say that on the dates mentioned in the plea of justification it would be shown by witnesses, whose testimony could not be shaken, that Euston had gone to Cleveland Street. Frank Hewett "was not now in this country" but the other person mentioned in the plea, John Saul, was "available to tell his story." At this point the cognoscenti among the spectators, who included some flamboyant representatives of Saul's "gay" world, stirred with excitement. There would be a star witness. Lockwood went on: "In July last, two persons — Veck and Newlove — were convicted in this court of a criminal offence with regard to this particular house. They were persons in a humble position of life, and their conviction caused little comment." (Their conviction, in fact, was in September, not July — a small mistake, but a portent of a larger sloppiness in the defense case.) Lockwood said that so far as Veck and Newlove were concerned the inquiry had been carried out with "an extraordinary amount of secrecy, for certainly few people are aware that the convictions had taken place." He then added a final sentence of some complexity which he hoped, no doubt, would impress the jury — he cannot have placed much hope in "Hanging" Hawkins. "If with those persons of humble origin persons of position have been associated, such as those mentioned in connection with the infamies of this house, I should be surprised to hear any argument suggesting that it is not in the interest of the public that names such as those should be published."

The defense then began to examine its witnesses, starting with John O'Loughlin, who was questioned by Asquith. O'Loughlin described himself as "coal dealer and green-grocer" and gave two addresses, one in Tottenham Street, the other in Saville Street. He was the first of several knockabout witnesses, who amused the more fashionable spectators with their quaint accents and odd slang. He said he had been talking to a Mr. Smith between seven and eight o'clock one night the previous summer, about May 20. They had been at the corner of Cleveland Street and Tottenham Street.

Asquith: "What did you see?"

Witness: "I was with Smith, and Smith says to me —"

"Never mind that. What did you see?"

"I saw a carriage drive up. The horse's head was opposite 23 Cleveland Street. A gentleman got out and knocked at 19."

"What happened then?" — "Nothing more, he went in."

"Have you seen the gentleman since?" — "Yes."

"Do you see him in court?" — "No. I saw him at Hyde Park Corner and I saw him outside this court."

"Look round the Court." — "My sight is very queer since."

"You have seen him since. Where?" — "At Hyde Park Corner around six weeks ago, and I have seen him twice since."

Lockwood then asked Euston to stand up. O'Loughlin said that he would like to see him walk (calling him "Mr. Euston"). Euston took a few steps and O'Loughlin had the spectators convulsed, which was not at all Lockwood's intention, when he announced: "I should say that is Lord Euston."

[147]

The Star reporter noted, "There was laughter at the witness's odd Irish manner." It was not very impressive as
evidence-in-chief — supposedly the cornerstone on which the
defense was building their case for justification. Russell had
little trouble in demolishing O'Loughlin on the grounds of
eyesight alone; O'Loughlin admitted that his sight had been
deteriorating for ten years and was getting "wusser" — a
usage that was sufficiently mid-Victorian and Dickensian to
raise another laugh. There was much emphasis on the questions of whether the carriage in which the gentleman had
arrived was a private one or not and whether it had been
drawn by one or two horses. O'Loughlin was not to be drawn
on such technicalities. "I know more about coal-barrows than
carriages," he replied.

On the occasion when O'Loughlin had seen Lord Euston
at Hyde Park Corner he had been posted there by a private
detective from an agency employed by Parke. He had heard
that this detective had previously been employed by *The
Times* to get up evidence against Parnell. The observation
produced more unhelpful laughter for the defense as it was
by then well known that the principal allegation against
Parnell — complicity in the Phoenix Park murders — had
been based on forged documents. (The exposure had been
made as a result of Sir Charles Russell's brilliant cross-
examination of the forger before the Parnell commission of
inquiry.)

O'Loughlin plowed on. Asked to describe the man he had
seen entering 19 Cleveland Street, he put the man's height at
between five feet nine inches and five feet ten inches; he was
good-looking, with a healthy complexion — "He did not look
like a man who had come out of hospital," volunteered the
witness.

Russell then diverted the witness to the issue of payment for his services, dealing first with his companion at Hyde Park Corner:

"What did this man give you for your trouble?"

"My cab fare home and a drink."

Russell continued pressing about payment but established nothing much beyond the meanness of private detectives. "Altogether," the witness had been paid less than ten shillings. One inquiry agent had not only failed to come across with a tip, but had actually borrowed "some baccy" from O'Loughlin, and also one shilling. There was more laughter when the witness commented, "He never returned either," and general merriment when Russell asked O'Loughlin to recall what was so distinctive about Lord Euston's walk.

"He was like an old policeman who had done twenty years on the stones — it was not a smart or nimble walk."

The next witness was John William Smith, a railway porter. He confirmed being with O'Loughlin and seeing Lord Euston getting out of a carriage outside 19 Cleveland Street in May. He had also seen him again going up to number 19 Cleveland Street only the previous week — on foot this time with no carriage or cab in sight. Euston was asked to stand up and Smith said, "That's the gentleman."

Pressed further, he said he thought he had seen Euston on six or seven occasions but might be wrong about the exact number of times because it had been at night. The major identification point he seized on had to do with Euston's trousers which were, he said, extremely wide — there was a "swell" fashion for wide bottoms — "His trousers were so loose that one leg of them would have made me a pair."

The man he had seen getting out of the carriage in May had been about his own height, five feet eight inches, or a little taller. Smith also had a distinct recollection of Lord Euston's moustache, which, however, "was not so curled today as on the previous occasion."

With their next witness, Michael O'Loughlin, son of John, the defense case began to lose some of its knockabout aspect and look distinctly seamy. Described as an unemployed barman, O'Loughlin seemed to regard his appearance in court as a chance to put on a show for the spectators. Russell began his cross-examination with a reprimand — "Leave your moustache alone" — and then pursued a long and heavy line of examination about O'Loughlin's successive jobs behind the bar. O'Loughlin's evidence was that he had been to Ascot for the Gold Cup two years previously and Lord Euston had been pointed out to him. Since then he had seen Euston "go in and come out of 19 Cleveland Street three or four times, at the end of May or the beginning of June." It was half-past eleven at night on one occasion; on another, about two in the morning. Three weeks before, he had seen Euston coming out of a house in Grosvenor Place. Like the other witnesses, Michael O'Loughlin had been recruited by Captain Webb of the Westminster inquiry office, though he admitted that when first shown a photograph of Lord Euston by a detective he did not say that he recognized him. He said it was nothing to do with anybody whether he did or not.

"Why?" asked Russell.

"Because it didn't suit me."

Russell then took up the theme of payment for his delayed identification.

Russell: "Have you received any money from Captain Webb or anyone else in connection with this matter?"

"No."

"Not a penny?" — "No."

"Have you been promised any?" — "No, but I expect I shall get some."

The pert answer had the spectators laughing, but the joke was again on the defense. The court then adjourned for lunch, which must have been eaten with most relish by the prosecution team. The defense witnesses, thus far, had provided rich entertainment but their lack of precision must have been galling for Mr. Parke and even worse for the image of Captain Webb's detective agency. None had apparently noticed that Lord Euston was six feet four inches tall.

At a time when people were generally much shorter than now — five feet seven or eight was regarded as tall — it was the most striking single thing about the man, yet none of the witnesses, when asked how they had recognized him, made the obvious reply: "I remember him because he was so tall." When the witnesses first saw the seated Euston they failed to see he was a giant — and amazingly Captain Webb and his band of detectives had not warned them. The witnesses, under the careful coaxing of Sir Charles Russell, disagreed about minor matters such as the color of Euston's clothes and said they remembered his moustache or the cut of his trousers, while the spectators watched with the delight of those who know a secret denied to others. (Russell was adept at such courtroom ploys. On another occasion, in a case where a claim for damages after injury was at issue, he asked the plaintiff to show the court "how well you could walk before the accident happened." The silly trick worked.)

The afternoon session opened a shade more promisingly for the defense. Hannah Elizabeth Morgan, a respectably dressed, middle-aged woman, said she had lived at 22 Cleveland Street, opposite number 19, for almost twelve months. She had noticed as many as fifty or sixty persons entering and leaving the house. In particular she had noticed one man — a tall man she had since recognized as Lord Euston when she had been driven by "a little dark gentleman," one of Captain Webb's private detectives, to Lord Euston's London home in Grosvenor Place.

Mrs. Morgan seemed a much more credible performer than the proceeding witnesses, though under Russell's cross-examination she was obliged to admit that of the many people she had seen milling around the Cleveland Street establishment the only one she could identify was Lord Euston. The fifth witness, Frederich Grant, another barman, emerged as a friend of the O'Loughlins. He recalled going to the music hall with John O'Loughlin around the end of May and, on returning around 11:30 P.M., noticing a gentleman coming out of number 19. O'Loughlin told him it was Lord Euston and told him about the character of the house. "I have seen the gentleman since and I see him now," said Grant, pointing to Lord Euston at the solicitor's table. Grant somewhat spoiled the effect, under cross-examination, by saying that he had not seen Lord Euston since that occasion, except in a photograph.

The drama of the appearance of the final defense witness was best captured by *The Star* reporter. "There was," he wrote, "a buzz of excitement when Mr. Lockwood spoke the name of his next witness — John Saul, a witness who had something more to speak than having seen Lord Euston go in and out of the house. Dramatic indeed was the situation when this young man, asked whether he recognised anyone in court as having been to Hammond's house, pointed to Lord Euston, and in his effeminate voice said distinctly: 'Yes, that one. I took him there myself.'

"It seemed minutes before another question was asked, so intense was the thrill which this declaration excited." Saul

[152]

must have been pleased with the effect as he pointed to Lord Euston.

"There is one gentleman I have brought home myself."

Lockwood: "Which is he?"

"That gentleman there with the moustache."

"Was that the first time he had been there, that person you took there?"

"Yes, I believe so."

"When was that?"

"Some time in April or May, 1887."

"Where did you meet this person?"

"In Piccadilly, between Albany courtyard and Sackville Street, near the Yorkshire Grey. He laughed at me and I winked at him. He turned sharp into Sackville Street."

"Who did?" — "The Duke, as we used to call him."

Lockwood: "Go on, and tell me what happened."

"The Duke, as we called him, came after me, and asked me where I was going. I said 'Home' and he said 'What sort is your place?'

" 'Very comfortable, I replied. He said 'Is it very quiet there?' I said 'Yes, it was', and then we had a hansom cab there. We got out by the Middlesex Hospital, and I took the gentleman to Cleveland Street, letting him in with my latch-key. I was not long in there, in the back-parlour or reception room, before Hammond came and knocked, and asked if we wanted any champagne or drinks of any sort, which he was in the habit of doing."

There was a titter of laughter in the courtroom. The solemnity of the proceedings was evidently in danger of complete collapse. Mr. Lockwood, addressing Justice Hawkins, expressed the hope that his task would not be made too difficult by such expressions of feeling. The whole thing was too horrible. The judge said that such levity was brutal and disgusting and he trusted it would not occur again. After giving further evidence — described by *The Times* court reporter as "of a character unfit for publication" — Saul went on to say that Lord Euston gave him a sovereign, leaving it on the chest of drawers.

"Did you see Lord Euston at the house again?"

"Once, and I did not forget it. Frank Hewett, who has, I believe, been sent abroad, and Newlove were both present on the occasion of Lord Euston's second visit. I complained to Hammond of his allowing boys in good position in the Post Office to be in the house while I had to walk the streets for what is in my face and that is shame." Only Saul would have taken advantage of such an occasion to start a trade union-style complaint about male prostitutes' working arrangements and unfair competition from post office boys. It was outrageous, but Saul played it to the hilt. *The Star* noted: "The Witness turned away from the court with a somewhat theatrical gesture."

Saul concluded his story of his relationship with Hammond by saying, "I quarreled with Hammond at the end of May 1887, though taking his mother's part, and then left him."

Sir Charles Russell rose to open his cross-examination in what a reporter described as "breathless silence."

Russell: "Where are you living now?"

Saul gave an address in Brixton, where, he said, he was being looked after by "a respectable man" called "Violet."

Russell wanted to know about the ring on his finger, a valuable gift, no doubt, from some rich protector. No, said Saul, the ring was paste. What about the silverheaded cane to which he seemed so attached? A bargain buy, said Saul, for 1s 6d in the Brixton Road. Russell then asked about the first evidence Saul had given. The answer produced a sensation.

"The first statement I made was at the Criminal Investigation Office to Inspector Abberline."

Saul went on to describe how he had later come into contact with Captain Webb's private inquiry office in Westminster. Captain Webb gave him half a sovereign a week pocket money "because I have to send money to my mother in Ireland who is very poor." Saul said that he knew Newlove and Hewett but none of the others on a list of post office employees produced by Russell. He was very sorry for Newlove. Hammond was getting a very good collection of post office boys at the time he had left.

Before Saul had gone to Cleveland Street with Lord Euston in the cab he had been unaware of the identity of his client. "I picked him up," Saul said, "just as I might have picked any other gentleman up." This one occasion he had spoken of was the only time he had communicated with Euston, directly or indirectly. Euston had warned him, "Be sure, if you see me, don't speak to me in the street." He had often seen the peer in public but observed instructions and never spoke to him.

Here was a witness who might have been made for Russell had he attempted to cover anything up. But it was hard to display forensic skill in discrediting a man who so comprehensively alienated the sympathy of both judge and jury every time he opened his mouth.

Russell moved onto the subject of Saul's "career of infamy." Saul had already admitted "infamy" in Dublin in 1875 and in London he had followed "the same infamous course of life."

"Did you do anything honest to earn your living?"

"Not much."

"What?"

"I worked hard at cleaning the houses of the gay people — the gay ladies on the beat, but I did not earn much."

Under further cross-examination, he said that one of the reasons for his quarrel with Hammond was that Hammond had charged him too much, and kept him hungry when he did not earn much. He admitted practicing "criminality" in other houses, but denied living with a woman who kept a brothel in the vicinity of Leicester Square. At one stage, he conceded, his residence had been a house in Nassau Street, near the Middlesex Hospital, "where vicious practices were carried on."

"Did you in Church Street live with a woman known as Queen Anne?"

"No, it is a man. Perhaps you will see him later on."

"Is he in attendance here then?"

"Yes sir. He is a young fellow who knows a lot of the aristocracy."

"Did you live with this man Grant, or Queen Anne, in Church Street, Soho?"

"No, he lived with me."

"And were you hunted out by the police?"

"No, they have never interfered. They have always been kind to me."

"Do you mean they have deliberately shut their eyes to your infamous practices?"

"They have had to shut their eyes to more than me."

Russell kept asking questions and Saul was perfectly happy to go on answering as long as he stayed in the limelight. Yes, he had offered evidence in the notorious Dublin Castle homosexual trials of the early 1880s. No, his contribution had not been rejected because he had been told that his word was not worthy of credit on oath; it had simply been old evidence. In this case he had been approached by Captain

Webb's office only after Parke had been committed for trial. No one had seen him earlier as he had been employed at the Drury Lane Theatre — Saul did not specify in what capacity, but, looking for an allusion as always, made a point of specifying the name of the production, *The Royal Oak*. When he had agreed to give evidence he had been ignorant of the fact that a considerable sum of money had been subscribed for Parke. Saul said he did not know Parke at all. He had offered himself as a witness only because he thought the editor was being treated very unfairly. Saul's support and expressions of sympathy were something the editor could have well done without, but the moment soon passed, and there was more excitement in court as Russell showed the witness a photograph of the peer.

"Do you recognise it?"

"Yes. You can tell him by his big white teeth and his moustache."

Saul insisted that on the two occasions when Euston had visited Cleveland Street he had been ignorant of his identity. He had learned it from a "friend called Carrington" (one of the "Mary-Annes" whose visiting card he had given to Abberline in August, and which still survives in the documents).

John Saul's hour of glory was coming to its end. Lockwood for the defense only kept him long enough to confirm once more that he had made a statement to Abberline — as if the conjuncture of Saul and the police made what he had said in court seem more authoritative.

Lord Euston then had the opportunity of putting his *poses plastiques* story more firmly on the record, and he comprehensively denied all Saul's allegations.

"What height are you?" asked Russell.

"Six feet four" replied Euston.

Lockwood found him virtually unshakable in cross-exami-

[157]

nation. The only modest achievement was establishing that Euston had been "thoroughly disgusted at being trapped into a place or caught in a place like that." That was why he had been reluctant "to talk about his own folly."

Lockwood: "Did you consider or not that the card you were given referred to some filthy exhibition?"

Euston: "I knew what *poses plastiques* were. I have seen some *poses plastiques* that you could not call filthy."

Lockwood: "Did you consider that the card referred to some kind of exhibition that you would be ashamed for it to be known amongst your friends that you had visited?"

Euston: "No, sir, I do not think I should have been so ashamed amongst my friends for that."

And so, with some formalized exchanges during which it was established that Euston knew Lord Arthur Somerset as a fellow member of the Turf Club — but denied either knowing he had recently left England or visiting him in Boulogne after his departure — the evidence was concluded. Since there had been no witnesses for the prosecution, other than Euston himself, Russell had the right of the last word to the jury. He used it to every advantage, stressing that they were "12 honest gentlemen." By the time he had finished it was growing late enough for the judge to say he would postpone his summing up until the following morning.

Lockwood asked for Parke's bail to be continued. This was granted, and Parke went home that night still a free man.

Mr. Justice Hawkins began his summing up by describing the libel as of "a very atrocious character which imputes to Lord Euston heinous crimes revolting to one's notions of all that is decent in human nature." He added that no one could exonerate himself from the consequences of such a libel "unless he is prepared to prove the truth of that which he alleges."

Euston, he continued, had submitted himself for cross-examination at the preliminary magistrates' court hearing, where no questions were put to him on any of the matters that had subsequently been given in evidence at the Old Bailey. Hawkins therefore agreed that Russell was right to exercise his discretion and call Euston last, and added that had he been in Russell's position he himself would have adopted the same course.

The judge moved next to the justification, beginning with the statement in the original article that Euston had gone to Peru, for which "there is not one particle of evidence." The defense had known this only too well and had made no mention of Peru at all either in its formal plea of justification or in the courtroom. Effectively, this point had been conceded. Hawkins then turned his attention to the matter of Euston's height. Here, he said, there had been "great and manifest discrepancies."

Witness after witness had persisted in describing Lord Euston as a man of middle height, whereas his height was exceptional, being six feet four inches. The evidence of John O'Loughlin was in many ways unreliable, and all the witnesses appeared to have been in communication with a private inquiry agency. The man Smith saw the visitor at Cleveland Street at the same time as O'Loughlin, but his evidence differed materially from that of the latter. O'Loughlin said Lord Euston wore a light suit, while Smith said he wore a dark frock coat. Smith, on the previous day, identified Lord Euston by what the witness had called "his very wide trousers," although he was wearing a long frock coat which almost concealed the trousers. The evidence of the younger O'Loughlin and his friend Grant was of a similar character.

Hawkins, in short, rejected the identification evidence and, given the omissions on the question of Euston's height, he had very little choice. The decision then largely turned on what John Saul had told the court. Here Hawkins felt he could indulge in some strong moral condemnation.

"A more melancholy spectacle, a more loathsome object" than the man Saul he never beheld. He hoped, for the honor of the Metropolitan Police, that it was not true, as Saul swore, that the police were kind to him. The jury had to weigh the oath of Lord Euston against the oath of Saul. He marveled much that the latter had not been prosecuted; on the contrary, he was accepted in a house and pampered on luxury which was denied to poor honest people. It made his blood hot within him as he heard the story. The creature said he had told Inspector Abberline his story in August last. If this were true, why did Abberline do nothing? He marveled again that there was not a warrant out for Lord Euston. As one of the public he would like to know why, if Abberline heard the story and believed it, nothing was done. If, on the other hand, the police knew the story to be false, he was not surprised at their apparent inactivity. Why was Newlove, who, according to Saul, could bear testimony against Lord Euston, not called? It was the duty of the defense to call him if his testimony could benefit the accused. In conclusion, Mr. Justice Hawkins charged the jury to return a verdict without fear or favor founded on the evidence they had heard and their intelligent appreciation of it.

His speech lasted two hours and twenty-five minutes. The jury was out for less than forty minutes. There was little doubt in anyone's mind. The foreman announced: "Guilty of Libel without justification."

Hawkins then gave Parke a chance. He offered to postpone sentence until the following morning if Parke either wished to communicate with his counsel or to submit anything himself. Lockwood replied that Parke did not want any post-

ponement. Hawkins then asked Parke if he himself had anything to add.

"I can only say I have acted in perfect good faith. What I
have published I believed to be in the public interest. I did
not, as has just been said by counsel appearing against me,
publish the libel without what I believed to be — and have
since found not to be — adequate evidence. What the evidence is I cannot state. Of course, I have been misled."

Parke was trying to have it both ways. Hawkins would not
allow it.

"Only mentioning it is not evidence. The libel is, I think I
may say — I do not mind telling you — exceedingly bad, but
if you would like to have until tomorrow to give me any
information which you think would alter my view of the matter you shall. But at present, as the evidence stands, I see
none that was in your possession at the time the libel was
published."

"I can only say that I had evidence at that time."

"I really must have more than that."

"I think it would be better for all parties under the circumstances if your Lordship would give the sentence now,"
Lockwood intervened.

"Very well," said Hawkins; and then, turning once more
to Parke, "And you think so too?"

"Yes, my Lord," Parke replied. "I cannot give you other
evidence without a breach of faith."

It was the traditional journalist's plea of the inviolability
of a source. Hawkins was not impressed.

"The plea that you could not produce this evidence without violating a source is one that I will never tolerate. If a
man chooses to take the responsibility of publication in his
newspaper, as you said that you were willing to do, he must
take the responsibility."

His sentence, he added, was meant both as a punishment to Parke and a warning to others "not to publish atrocious libels on others without justification."

"You will go to prison for 12 months without hard labour."

Ernest Parke really found out who his friends in the press were after the verdict. They divided as in most cases, as one might expect, on political lines, with the more radical newspapers still championing, or at least expressing sympathy for Parke. The Tory press for the most part exulted in the proper conviction of a troublemaker. *The Star* led the sympathetic contingent:

We know Mr Parke personally, and we know him as an honourable high-minded man. With a more than ordinary desire to advance the public welfare, of strong and intense convictions, he goes into every project with ardour and fearlessness, and the action he took in the case which has ended so disastrously for him was dictated, we know, by his sense of his duty as a journalist. We can honour the motives which induced Mr Parke to remain silent when challenged to give the grounds which led to his original action, but we think that he pushed chivalry too far.

The British Weekly echoed the same thought, but was more severe on Lord Euston. The very idea of *poses plastiques* evidently boggled the editorial mind:

Every really pure and just mind must be shocked by the ferocious severity of the sentence passed upon Mr Parke. No one can doubt the purity of his motives, and any error into which he has been betrayed by his zeal for social morality could have been sufficiently christened by less than twelve months' imprisonment which involves hard labour and the utmost degradation. If the man whom he had libelled were deserving

[162]

of sympathy, there would be more excuse for the extreme penalty. But Lord Euston made confessions which, while they did not justify Mr Parke's charge, were of a most disgraceful character.

A more surprising source of comfort to the afflicted editor came from the Tory *St Stephen's Review* which was "sorry for Mr Parke," who, in reality, "did no more than thousands of gossips about town were doing every day. Each one of these gossips is just as worthy of punishment as Mr Parke. He had the misfortune to put his on paper, so he gets a year's imprisonment; the others go free and continue their observations. He has borne on him the inequity of them all — if one man in all humility paraphrase a Scriptural quotation."

W. T. Stead's *Pall Mall Gazette*, which had been oddly reticent about the whole affair after breaking the first story about an aristocratic connection with 19 Cleveland Street, made a plea for reduction of sentence on "a young journalist of promise and good faith," on the grounds:

1. That the only signal example made by our courts is in the case not of a man guilty of the crimes, but of one who, however rashly and mistakenly, endeavoured to drag the crimes into the light of the day.
2. That, accordingly, the severity of the sentence was a grave mistake in the public interest.
3. That Lord Euston admitted that he went to the house on a disgraceful errand, though it was not the worse errand which Mr Parke attributed to him.
4. That Mr Parke had at least one deposition when he made the charge.

The Daily Telegraph, in contrast, came to the conclusion that the character of Lord Euston was "entirely cleared," and added: "The condemnation of Parke to imprisonment for twelve calendar months prevents for that time, and perhaps for all future time, a foul-mouthed slanderer from inflicting any further injury on society and poisoning the very air we breathe."

The Saturday Review congratulated Lord Euston "for having grappled with and abated one of the most loathsome and scandalous nuisances of any time and country. Mr Parke's profession, as has been decided in a court of justice, is to minister to a foul taste with fouler lies; and he deserves as much mercy as a polecat. Nay, he deserves much less; for, after all, the polecat did not choose its peculiarities, does not stink or murder for notoriety or for lucre, and, above all, does not pretend that its practices are 'for the public benefit.'"

The People also thought "Lord Euston has earned the gratitude of society for enabling the law to stamp upon a miscreant who, if he had his deserts, should be whipped at the cart's tail from one end of London to the other."

The Echo, which fully reported the trial and all that preceded it, and advertised the affair freely on its contents bills, said Mr. Parke libeled Lord Euston "more to float a small local print, and to increase the notoriety of a daily paper with which he was conspicuously connected, than to vindicate the law or to promote social purity."

The unkindest cut was made by *The Labour Elector,* the official paper of the London dockers whose struggles in the previous year had been manfully defended by Parke's *North London Press.* In the considered opinion of *The Labour Elector*'s editorial writer: "If Lord Euston had gone to the [newspaper] office and there and then physically twisted the little wretch's neck nobody would have blamed him. We are not, as a rule, in favour of Lynch Law, but there are undoubtedly cases in which it is permissible, and this was one. Penal servitude for life or for a lengthened period of years might have met the justice of the case; but twelve months' imprisonment, without hard labour, is little better than a mockery."

On January 25, 1890, *The North London Press*, bereft of its editor and proprietor, published its last issue. It had been in existence for little over a year, but its passing was a significant loss to British journalism. Parke had been in the thick of the various working-class struggles both as an editor and speaker. He had helped start a union for underpaid postmen; championed John Burns, the dockers' leader; exposed the callous exploitation of their agents by insurance companies; and struck a refreshingly modern note in his attitude to Mr. Stanley's exploits in Africa (while most papers lauded the journalist-explorer as "a pioneer of civilisation," the tiny *North London Press* was most impressed by "his unscrupulousness and savage methods" that made the native population "pray that civilisation heralded by such pioneers may be checked upon its road").

Frank Harris, the editor of *The Fortnightly Review*, was acquainted with both Lord Euston and Ernest Parke, whom he considered "a convinced Radical and a man of high character." Parke had complained to Harris that all that he had done was to reproduce the substance of a statement made to a police inspector which in his view should have been privileged. Harris endorsed this view and condemned the sentence as "infamous and vindictive," suggesting that Justice Hawkins, under pressure from an ambitious wife, had imposed the "preposterous penalty" in order to please his superiors and speed his ennoblement. Harris, as usual, tended to overcompress the facts. Hawkins still had another nine years to wait for his peerage, though it was true that his wife, a noted Mrs. Malaprop, was unusually ambitious for her husband. (She is reported to have said after being congratulated on

[165]

possession of a particularly fine Persian carpet: "You wouldn't believe how many people have copulated me on that carpet.")

No conspiracy theories are necessary to account for either the verdict on Parke or the sentence. His defense had been a shambles and on the evidence before the court neither judge nor jury could reasonably have acted other than they did. In his excellent book, *Their Good Names*, H. Montgomery Hyde, the biographer of Lord Birkett, carefully reassesses the trial evidence and finds no substantiation for Harris's criticisms. It is difficult to fault this assessment, yet the case did leave a number of important questions unanswered.

Unfortunately, further research — like so much of the trial evidence — has tended to turn up facts that are inconclusive. Michael Harrison, the biographer of Prince Albert Victor, recently unearthed some intriguing information in the rate books of the time. These show that for the period from midsummer 1888 to midsummer 1889, the rates of Charles Hammond in 19 Cleveland Street were paid by a Michael O'Loughlin, presumably the son of the first identification witness against Lord Euston and friend of most of the others. Harrison, however, puts this fact — interesting though it is — at the service of a very large conspiracy theory indeed, which involved "the connivance of both prosecution and defence." In Harrison's view, the whole trial was part of a complex plot to "take the heat off Prince Eddy" in which Lord Euston was chosen to act the part of the libeled man on account of his magnificent heterosexual track record. Parke, in brief, was set up, gulled into a libel that would discredit the Press generally and stop the flow of "revelations."

It is a handsome theory but one that requires a more substantial volume of fact than has yet become available. The documents that have recently been opened to inspection at the Public Records Office are helpful only up to a point. It is, for example, still a mystery why Parke failed to call Newlove to corroborate Saul's evidence, a failure which, as we have seen, was commented on by the judge. The records show that Parke's solicitor was granted permission by the Home Office to visit Newlove in jail and that the solicitor requested copies of his (and the other boys') depositions. This request was refused, though the solicitor was informed that he might subpoena for any documents that might help his client. It is clear from the internal evidence of *The North London Press* stories that Parke must have obtained his original information from a sight or knowledge of Newlove's deposition and not from John Saul (Saul made no mention of Lord Arthur Somerset in his statement to Inspector Abberline). Yet Newlove, potentially a far more credible witness than Saul, was not called, nor was his deposition subpoenaed. At the very least they would have shown that Frank Hewett, who Newlove knew very well, was not a figment of Saul's fertile imagination.

There is a further mystery which again worked to Parke's disadvantage at the trial. The judge in his summing up clearly implied that the reason Inspector Abberline never moved against Lord Euston after taking down Saul's statement was because the police believed it was untrue. The recently disclosed documents establish that this was not necessarily the case. Abberline still suspected Euston but did not feel he had sufficient evidence. On November 25, ten weeks after taking Saul's statement, Abberline put in a memorandum to Commissioner Monro requesting permission to take two of the post office boys — Thickbroom and Swinscow — to Parke's committal hearing at Bow Street. The object was to see if they could identify the plaintiff, Lord Euston. The request was passed on to the Attorney General, Sir Richard Webster, who was not at all keen on the idea. "We should," he wrote, "keep aloof from the present proceedings."

There is one explanation — theory is perhaps too large a word — that can tie most of these puzzling facts together. It does not have the grandeur of Mr. Harrison's conspiracy but there are conspiratorial elements in it. It revolves around two of the hardest facts: Parke's refusal to reveal his other "source" besides Saul's statement, and Abberline's determination to nail Lord Euston as well as Lord Arthur Somerset. Either directly or through third parties, Parke must have been doing a deal with the police. After all the frustration of trying to mobilize the case against Lord Arthur Somerset, Abberline may well have been tempted to take a shortcut with Lord Euston. Essentially, Parke did nothing more than publish the names in Newlove's original statement (unfortunately for Harrison's theory, long before the first breath of royal scandal). But this must have been enough for Abberline's purposes which would be to strengthen his case against Lord Euston. If Euston did not sue, it would be construed as evidence against him; if he did, the newspaper might turn up fresh facts for its own case and give its own witnesses a chance to identify the suspect. At worst, if he sued and won handsomely, it was no skin off Abberline's nose provided Parke did not disclose his source. Parke never did.

The police could afford to let Parke have Saul, who did not affect the one solid case they had — or thought they had — against Lord Arthur Somerset. But Newlove was a different matter; they would need his evidence if Lord Arthur were ever brought to trial. Meanwhile, they would not want to see his evidence tainted by its delivery in a controversial and highly publicized libel action.

Did Abberline feed Parke the totally false information about Lord Euston's departure for Peru? We can, on the

10 LEFT The young Prince Albert Victor ("Eddy"), Heir Presumptive to the English throne, with his sister, Princess Maud.

11 BELOW A studio portrait of Prince Albert Victor, taken in the late 1880s when he was directly menaced by the Cleveland Street scandal, earned him the malicious nickname "Mr. Collar and Cuffs."

12 ABOVE Lord Arthur Somerset, royal equerry and "client" of the Cleveland Street brothel, fled the country to escape justice and protect the reputation of the royal family.

13 ABOVE Sir Francis (later Lord) Knollys, private secretary to the Prince of Wales, proved himself an adept "fixer" of royal scandals, sexual and otherwise.

14 BELOW Frank (later Sir Frank) Lockwood, Liberal MP, was defense counsel for journalist Ernest Parke, who attacked the Establishment's version of the case. Later Lockwood was appointed Solicitor-General.

15 BELOW Lord Halsbury is shown here in a *Vanity Fair* cartoon of the right-wing Lord Chancellor whose influence, as the Crown's chief legal officer, was exercised on the side of concealment.

16 RIGHT Sir Dighton Probyn, war hero and member of the royal household, who helped deflect suspicion from the monarchy by alerting Lord Arthur Somerset. He was later promoted to Field-Marshal.

17 BELOW A brilliant advocate whose services assisted the cover-up in two court cases involving principals in the affair, Sir Charles Russell was later promoted to Lord Chief Justice.

18 RIGHT In a portrait taken soon after he became
king, and acquired the style Edward the Peace-
maker, Edward VII is wearing the famous Homburg
hat, which he popularized in England.

19 BELOW This late nineteenth-century engraving
of the post office boys' locker room and kitchen
shows the telegraph boys. (Off-duty services for the
aristocratic "clients" of Cleveland Street were
provided by such boys.)

present evidence, only conjecture, but Abberline, as we have seen, was a resourceful and determined detective. If there was one thing that must have persuaded Euston of the excellence of his chances at law it must have been this gratuitous reference to his "flight." It is difficult to imagine Parke inserting such a damaging detail, so easily capable of disproof, without its coming from an authoritative source. If Abberline were responsible, it would not be the first time the police "managed" the news in order to flush out a suspect.

There is also a hint of a further subplot in the newspapers of the time. *The Star*, for example, was particularly censorious of: "Those who encouraged him [Parke] in the publication of his attack on Lord Euston. If we had such a responsibility we should not feel easy until we had purged our souls by revealing our personality and so bear the share of the punishment to which we had brought another person." The well-informed London correspondent of *The New York Herald* stated his view that Parke was "a catspaw for a better known journalist who did not want to publish in his own paper." The "better known journalist" never stood up to be publicly counted. But the gossip and a deal of powerful circumstantial evidence pointed in the direction of the decade's most famous muckraker, W. T. Stead of *The Pall Mall Gazette*. Stead had the motive: an abiding interest in the subject dating back to the homosexual dossier he compiled for Labouchere's benefit in 1885. His police contacts were excellent. His paper was the first to "break" the story of Cleveland Street, albeit in guarded terms. *The Gazette* then demurely sat on the sidelines of the affair until it made its plea for clemency after Parke's trial. It is easy to see why W. T. Stead, having previously served three months in jail for his earlier services to vice exposure, would not be anxious to run the risk of a longer term when the Cleveland Street scandal developed. At the same time, Stead, through his police and parliamentary contacts, must have been among the best informed on its progress. It was (and is) almost standard procedure of the editorial freemasonry to pass on information of "public interest" to another newspaper if, for some reason, it could not be accommodated in the columns of the paper that originally obtained it. And *The North London Press* could hardly have been considered a circulation rival of *The Pall Mall Gazette*.

Parke's conviction effectively marks the end of the newspapers' enthusiasm for the scandal. For its part, the government took pains not to do anything that might reawaken the press's appetite. It was, for example, evident after the Parke trial that Saul must be considered liable to prosecution for perjury. On January 31, Sir Augustus Stephenson dutifully but with scant enthusiasm referred the matter to Sir Richard Webster, asking whether Saul should be prosecuted, either for perjury or sodomy. On February 3, the Attorney General replied with a firm opinion against any prosecution.

A consensus was beginning to emerge, both within the Government and among the main organs of opinion, that the scandal should be allowed to die a natural death. There was, however, one flamboyant figure outside the consensus— Henry Labouchere, the M.P. for Northampton. And he still had a dramatic card to play.

NINE

Calling the Prime Minister
a Liar

The conviction of Ernest Parke produced no evidence of repentance in Labouchere. He had no particular quarrel with the verdict, but saw it as irrevelant to the main issue. Nor was he much impressed by the issue of a summons on Lord Arthur Somerset's solicitor, Arthur Newton, and his two legmen, Taylerson and De Gallo. They were in his view scapegoats for higher authority. "I would suggest to the public prosecutor," Labouchere wrote in *Truth*, "that he should at once obtain summons against Lord Salisbury and Mr Matthews for seeking to defeat the ends of justice in the matter of the Cleveland Street scandal. . . ."

It was becoming increasingly clear to Labouchere that the task of unraveling and exposing what he now considered a massive cover-up by the authorities was beyond the resources of the press. *Truth* was a handy weapon for sparking controversy but incapable of creating the kind of explosion he had in mind. The only effective place for the blast was inside the House of Commons; the timing required some thought but he had no doubt that an occasion would arise.

Labouchere was a past master at exploiting parliamentary rules and technicalities for his own ends. On one occasion he had actually taken advantage of a near-empty House of Commons — it was the dinner hour — to push through an anti-Government vote abolishing the power of veto of the House of Lords, a measure that was not finally enacted until 1911. Labouchere's ruse was, in fact, not much more than a gesture, since his "vote" was easily reversed. However it embarrassed and enraged the Salisbury administration which had been made to look foolish.

On Friday, February 28, 1890, the House of Commons was in committee session to consider the annual vote on the Civil Service estimates, normally a dry statistical occasion in the parliamentary calendar attracting only a handful of members. After a brief desultory debate, the formal question was put that a sum not exceeding £3,725,103 be granted on account to defray charges for the Civil Service and Revenue departments.

Labouchere then rose to move the reduction of the appropriation, basing his motion on the fact that certain officials whose salaries were included in it had conspired together to defeat the course of justice.

At fifty-eight he was probably at the height of his debating powers — a gray-bearded, distinctly tubby figure with a placid, slightly bland gaze and a deceptively mild drawl that he employed when delivering the epigrams that earned him the reputation of being "England's greatest wit since Sheridan."

He began speaking at 5:20 P.M. and although the violence of his denunciations amazed his fellow M.P.s, his chosen subject came as no surprise. Word rapidly got around, and the House — unusually well attended to start with — rapidly filled up. By the time Labouchere had finished one of the finest speeches ever delivered in the Commons, a masterpiece of eloquence and analysis which took him one hour precisely, the benches were crammed. At 7:45 P.M. when the Radical member for Northampton was suspended from the House because he had called the Prime Minister a liar, there were 273 M.P.s in the lobbies. It was the kind of turnout usually reserved for set-piece occasions like the speech from the Throne or the debate on the Budget.

Labouchere's opening was clear enough. "There has been a gross scandal, and there is ground for investigation into the conduct of those who are responsible for it." His first complaint concerned the speed with which Veck and Newlove had been tried and the lightness of their sentences (of nine and four months, respectively). Labouchere maintained that Newlove and Veck had received mild sentences because of an agreement between the prosecution and the defense — the more serious charges had been dropped in return for a guilty plea on the minor ones. "The committee," he said, "will remember how if a poor man, urged by a primary necessity, steals some small thing, he is sent to prison often for more than nine months. . . . [I]t is pretty clear that the real object of this trial was to stop all further disclosures, hush the matter up."

Labouchere went on: "The matter occurred in the Post Office and they — I honour and respect them for it — insisted that action should be taken. The Solicitor to the Treasury who is under the orders of the Home Secretary, knew perfectly well by this time that certain names had been mentioned; and they determined, so far as they were concerned, that if they were obliged to prosecute these men the case should go no further if they could prevent it."

It was outrageous that these two comparatively subaltern figures (Newlove and Veck) should have found themselves behind bars while Hammond, who after all had run the brothel, had been allowed to skip the country, take his ease with a boyfriend on the continent, and then in his own good time embark on the *Pennland* at Antwerp for a new life in America. It was not the fault of the police, Labouchere said; in fact, they had been pressing for Hammond to be extradited since the second week of July. Their request had gone from the police to the Home Office to the Treasury to the Foreign Office (over which, as Foreign Secretary, presided the Marquess of Salisbury). On July 25 his decision had been handed down; it was Salisbury who had decided that Hammond should be left where he was, and thus it was ultimately Salisbury's responsibility that he had not been prosecuted.

It was obvious that Labouchere had studied the case very carefully and had official sources of information. He was now well into his stride and commanded the attention of the House without interruption. Attorney General Sir Ronald Webster, who in due course was to reply to Labby's accusations, took notes on the Government benches but made no comment. He was evidently waiting to see how full a case Labouchere had managed to assemble.

The Radical member continued with his chronology. On September 16 the Secretary to the Post Office wrote to the police, urging that immediate action should be taken against Hammond who was then in Belgium — or otherwise he would disappear. The police wasted no time in passing this on to the Treasury, who replied on the following day that there was no evidence justifying extradition. The inevitable happened and Hammond flew the coop.

Labouchere continued: "During the time he had been in Belgium the Belgian police reported that he had been accompanied by an English boy. This boy had been abstracted from his parents, presumably for vile purposes. Now, while Hammond was in Belgium, whilst the English and Belgian police were surrounding him, a Mr Newton, who was the solicitor to Lord Arthur Somerset, and also Veck and Newlove, either himself went to Belgium or sent someone who not only gave Hammond a large sum in cash but also paid the fare of the boy who had fallen into such a terrible position."

Webster: "Who obtained the tickets?"

Labouchere obviously did not know the answer to this question but he had no intention of allowing the Attorney General to distract him with debating points. He kept going. "I cannot help thinking that if the Government had been in earnest they might have obtained extradition. Our Extradition Treaties with both France and Belgium cover such charges as indecent assault, either by the principal or by accessories. It was put in evidence before the magistrate, and I do not think it was questioned, that Hammond induced boys to come to his house, that he took them into a room, and had them sold to the creatures who were going to assault them. . . ."

Having disposed of Hammond, Labouchere moved on to Lord Arthur Somerset and began to spell out the case against him, adding that "in no other city in the world would it be possible to find the abominations of Cleveland Street carried out so openly."

Lord Arthur Somerset had been identified by the boys on 23 July. On 23 August Allies had made his statement which included the evidence of the postal orders he had received from Knightsbridge Post Office (the location was important since the post office was opposite the cavalry barracks where the Prince of Wales's equerry had been identified in the first place). Although the police had kept the Treasury informed of the progress their case was making, they at first received no instructions at all, thus allowing Lord Arthur to pursue his life as usual. The object of the Treasury, said Labouchere, had been to hush up the matter, not to have any further prosecutions.

Lord Arthur Somerset went abroad but was back by October 8, the day his grandmother, the Dowager Duchess of Beaufort, was buried on the Badminton estate. The Post Office police, still trying to get their man, heard about this and sent a constable down to Badminton in the hope of arresting Lord Arthur. The Treasury promptly instructed the police to call their man off at once, and they had no choice except to obey their orders.

Labouchere then turned his guns on the Prime Minister and Foreign Secretary, Lord Salisbury. Sir Dighton Probyn, a general, a V.C., and one of the Prince of Wales's most important advisors, had, according to Labouchere's information, asked for an interview with the Prime Minister by telegram "about the middle of October, and on October 18 the two men met.

"Sir Dighton Probyn was informed that a warrant for Lord Arthur Somerset was due and Somerset then fled the country. I ask Honourable Members was it the business of a Prime Minister and Foreign Secretary to mix himself up in such matters?"

Labouchere found it horrifying that the fugitive Lord Arthur should still have been officially a major in the British army when he had presented himself to the Sultan of Constantinople to offer his services as a military expert. When public attention had been drawn to the case, ministers, fearing a mess, had looked about for a Jonah to feed to the whale of public opinion and found him in Mr. Newton, Lord Arthur Somerset's solicitor, whom they prosecuted.

The sum of these facts, Labouchere declared, amounted to "a criminal conspiracy by the very guardians of public morality and law with the Prime Minister at their head."

Then, in what the Commons recognized as a reference to Prince Albert Victor, Labouchere made a severe comment on "foreign newspapers" in which the name of "a gentleman of high position" was mentioned. He was "absolutely certain" that there was no foundation for "the calumny" on this individual. In connection with this he wished to add that a still more eminent gentleman (the Prince of Wales) had used all his efforts to fully publicize the case, and it had been due to his efforts that the government had been forced to the qualified action it had taken against Lord Arthur Somerset. Labouchere reminded members that he had strong views on the subject of royal grants, but he expressed his opinions openly. He protested against the good name of any man — "be he Prince or peasant" — being whispered and hinted away.

Labouchere made a final plea for an official investigation of the affair, in accordance with his original motion, before begging to move a reduction of the Civil Service appropriation by a token £100.

Sir Richard Webster, the Attorney General, was the image of outrage. This was a very special day for him as well as Labouchere: "Of all occasions I have spoken in the House and of all the questions I have heard raised since I have had the honour of being a Member of this House, nothing in my opinion has approached the importance of this occasion or the charge made by the honourable member of Northampton. He has charged the Prime Minister with being a party to a criminal conspiracy to defeat the ends of justice."

The House should remember, said Sir Richard, that Labouchere's infamous charges were also leveled against himself, the Treasury Solicitor, possibly the Commissioner of Police, and, what was to him much more important, it was suggested that members of his own profession who had practiced for years and those whose names were well known had also been mixed up in that foul conspiracy with their knowledge. The case had been put into the hands of the Treasury Solicitor on July 25. From that time down to the present every step in the proceedings had been taken under his direction.

There was, he said, no truth in the allegation that Veck and Newlove's mild punishment was the result of a "wicked and corrupt bargain." In support of his contention, the Attorney General read out a statement by Henry Poland, Q.C., the prosecuting counsel at the trial, to the effect that "I wish to say that I neither directly nor indirectly made any arrangements with the prisoners' counsel as to what counts the prisoners should plead guilty to, and that there was no undertaking of any kind, either expressed or implied, as to what should be done by me or the prisoners' counsel."

Turning to the issue of extradition, the Attorney General first asked if Labouchere would give him the authority for the statement that Lord Salisbury had sent a letter, on July 25, saying that Hammond could not be extradited. Labouchere shook his head, evidently not ready to disclose his source.

"Then how has it come to this," asked Sir Richard, "that without any warrant at all such charges can be made across the floor of the House?" There were cheers from the Government side at this ostensibly bold assertion of righteous indignation. Sir Richard went on to say that "as a matter of fact" the letter was written by one of the official secretaries in the Foreign Office, it being a matter of routine business. He would not go into the strictly legal aspects of the matter, but the only ground on which Hammond's extradition could have been demanded was aggravated or indecent assault; unfortunately, in his case all the boys consented and were above the protected age.

As far as Lord Arthur Somerset was concerned, Sir Richard did not mind telling the House that he was concerned about the corroborative testimony and "had not altogether trusted" his own judgment on the matter. He then told members about the two private consultations with the Lord Chancellor in August and October.

There was a loud "oh" from Labouchere; this was clearly something his source either had not known or had not told him.

The Attorney General then dealt with Labouchere's assertion that the post office boys had not been fully examined before the magistrate. Sir Richard again had the Tory benches cheering with his flat denial: no word ever passed between him and Mr. Avory and the Treasury Solicitor as to the questions to be put. The statements were taken and examined in the ordinary way. Sir Richard was shocked at Labouchere's implication that questions ought to have been asked "by means of a side wind, so to speak, in order to elucidate a charge against another person." That would have been "most discreditable."

Sir Richard then attempted to deal with the thorny question of the Prime Minister's interview with Sir Dighton Probyn. By now the Attorney General had discovered Labouchere's weakest point — his reluctance to reveal his sources publicly — and he exploited it to the full: "Lord Salisbury says that he made no reference to the date of the issue of the warrant against Lord Arthur Somerset." He then challenged Labouchere to produce the name of his informant.

Labouchere said he was prepared to write the name down on a piece of paper but it would be up to the Attorney General to decide whether it should be read to the House. The offer was not taken up, being somehow lost in a rising crescendo of assertion and counterassertion. The Attorney General had Lord Salisbury's word that mention of an imminent warrant against Lord Arthur Somerset had not been made by the Prime Minister. In any case a warrant was not then being prepared; the Attorney General had not given instructions for its issue until early November. Labouchere, unimpressed, hotly contested this version of events.

Webster: "Will the honourable member pardon me? I stated distinctly that Lord Salisbury denied the allegation about the warrant. He said nothing whatever about the date of issue of the warrant."

Labouchere: "The honourable gentleman thought he had proved his case by asking, from whom did you get this information? I offered to write it down and submit it to the honourable and learned gentleman, and if he, having seen the name, liked to read it to the House he was at full liberty to do so. I can perfectly well understand why the honourable and learned gentleman did not accept the proposal. I am obliged to speak frankly and truly in this matter. I assert, if I am obliged to do it, that I do not believe Lord Salisbury."

The House was in an uproar. It was an allegation that Mr. Courtney, chairman of the Estimates Committee, felt had to be withdrawn.

Courtney: "It would be intolerable for an honourable

member to use that language of a member of this House, and he cannot be permitted to use it of a member of the other House of Lords."

Labouchere: "I repeat it."

Courtney: "I call upon the honourable gentleman to withdraw."

Labouchere: "I decline to do so."

After ten minutes of to-ing and fro-ing on points of order, W. H. Smith, who, as first Lord of the Treasury, was the senior member of the Government present, moved that Labouchere should be expelled for refusing to follow the direction of the Chair. T. P. O'Connor, the M.P. for Liverpool, a Radical ally of Labouchere's and a fellow supporter of Home Rule for Ireland, tried his hand at running a little interference for the Northampton member. He, in effect, also called Salisbury a liar and then noted that the Chair had not acted in expelling him although he was apparently as vulnerable as Labouchere who had now withdrawn from the Chamber. It was a lost cause. The vote on Labouchere's suspension went against him by 177 to 96.

He was able to make only one more brief appearance at eight o'clock when the ruling was confirmed and he was required to withdraw again, undergoing a one-week suspension. He accepted the inevitable. "I beg, Sir, to withdraw, expressing at the same time my regret that my conscience would not allow me to say I believed Lord Salisbury. . . ."

The debate continued with Labby briefing his supporters as best he could from the smoking room. It was obviously hopeless as he was the only member, with the possible exception of Webster, who really knew the facts of the case. Nonetheless his allies did their best. Mr. E. Robertson, the radical member for Dundee, was the first speaker, at 8:10 P.M.

"An ancient privilege of this House, the liberty of debate,

has been infringed, when a Member of this house is expelled for declaring he did not believe the word of an individual who happened to be a member of the other House."

At 8:37 P.M. the Radical member for Newcastle-upon-Tyne, John Morley, tried unsuccessfully to move that the debate should be continued when Labouchere's suspension expired.

At 9:22 P.M. T. P. O'Connor was back again, and by now the success of the Government's strategy was established. No one, apart from Labouchere, knew enough to challenge the denials.

I must congratulate the Attorney-General on the success of his tactics . . . by provoking my Hon. friend into an assertion as to his credence or want of credence regarding Salisbury's utterance.

If the Government are desirous of snatching a verdict under these circumstances, let them do so, but they will have to face the verdict that will be given outside this House. It will be for the country to judge the Government forcing this question to a premature vote when the House has before it only an imperfect statement of the real facts.

When a humble person is charged with such an offence, does the Attorney-General consult the Lord Chancellor and the Prime Minister? There is no answer to the fact that the titled position of suspected persons induced consultations with ministers of the Crown who would not otherwise have been consulted. Is that equality before the law? Is the prosecution of a crime like this because a man happens to bear a title to be made a Cabinet question?

O'Connor was struck by the singular coincidence that Lord Arthur Somerset's flight and the interview between Lord Salisbury and Sir D. Probyn should coincide. And, like several other Irish members, he was indignant about the events of the Badminton funeral, a touchy issue since in Ireland the funerals of patriots had notoriously become occasions for police arrests. "Constable Hanks was sent to arrest Lord Arthur Somerset on the day of the funeral of the Dowager Duchess Beaufort — but why when he got to Badminton were his orders countermanded? I would suggest out of kindness — it would have been an ungracious thing to do to arrest a man at a funeral. But no such considerations enter into the Irish administration. We know that Irish funerals are happy hunting grounds not only for arrests but for baton charges too."

There was another Irish matter hanging over the debate — sore memories of the letter forged by Richard Pigott which had appeared in *The Times* and claimed to show that the Irish leader Parnell, a close friend of Labouchere's, had approved of the Phoenix Park murders. Lord Salisbury had at one stage claimed that the letter was genuine and, although it was later proved to be forged and Pigott committed suicide, the damage to Parnell's reputation had been severe. (It was Labouchere, incidentally, who contributed to the support of the dead man's family, and Labby to whom he had turned when the plot misfired. It was characteristic of Labby's generosity that he had behaved so well towards a man who had been a virulent political opponent and helped set back the cause which was perhaps uppermost in his mind, Home Rule for Ireland, by thirty-odd years.)

As the evening wore on, members who had consumed too much wine at dinner arrived to add their contributions, but the heart had long since gone out of the debate. It dragged on until after midnight, and at 12:10 A.M. the Government got their majority, 206 members supporting them and only 66 voting against. There would be no inquiry and Labouchere's motion to reduce the Civil Service budget was rejected.

The postscript to it came in the House of Lords on Monday, March 3, when the Marquess of Salisbury made his own statement which read as follows:

I see my conduct has been called in question in the other House. My Lords, it is said that I met Sir Dighton Probyn with the view of enabling a person who was exposed to a serious charge to escape from justice. My meeting with Sir Dighton Probyn happened in this wise. I was coming from France, I think it was on the eighteenth of October, and when I landed at Dover I found a telegram from Sir Dighton Probyn asking if he could see me in London. I had no notion what it was about — I imagined it had something to do with Foreign Office business connected with the journeys of the Prince of Wales. I replied that I should be passing through Town, and that he would find me at the Great Northern Railway Station in time for the seven o'clock train. I missed the seven o'clock but I arrived in time for the half past seven and Sir Dighton Probyn came to me there. He then informed me what he wanted to do was to ask me whether there was any ground for certain charges which had been made in the newspapers against sundry persons whom he named. My reply was, that so far as I knew, there was no ground for any of them, no vestige of evidence against anyone except one person, whose name it is not necessary to mention, and I said that, as against that person, that the evidence was not thought to be sufficient in the judgement of those whose business it was to decide. I think I added — but of that I am not quite certain — that rumours had reached me that further evidence had been obtained, but I did not know what its character was. My Lords, I am not ashamed to say that is all I recollect of a casual interview for which I was in no degree prepared, to which I did not attach the slightest importance, and of which I took no notes whatsoever. The train started very soon afterwards.

The interview was brief and hurried, and, as far as I know, the rest of the conversation principally consisted of expressions on the part of Sir Dighton Probyn of absolute disbelief in the charges which were levelled against the person whom I have indicated, and of answers of a more reserved character on my part. I cannot give your Lordships any positive information as to the precise language that was used at the interview; but I can give you negative information. I am quite certain that I never said, as had been imputed to me, that a warrant was about to be issued the next day, because such a statement would have been absolutely inconsistent with what I am certain I did say, that, in the judgement of the legal authorities, the evidence was insufficient. You cannot issue a warrant against a person if the evidence is insufficient. I certainly conveyed no secrets to Sir Dighton Probyn, for the best of all possible reasons, that I had no secrets to convey. I had been abroad, and I had no further information except mere rumour of the precise condition in which the affair stood; and I may add that I can aver in the most confident manner that the suggestion which has been made that a man of Sir Dighton Probyn's character and career could have appointed an interview with me for the purpose of defeating the ends of justice is the wildest and most malignant imagination that has ever been conceived.

For the rest, my Lords, the subject is not one that lends itself to extensive treatment, or that commends itself for lengthened debate; but I thought it right to say these few words, in order to give any noble lords who might wish to avail themselves of the opportunity of questioning me on the matter should they desire to do so. To this House I am responsible, and I desire to act fully up to the responsibility.

It was in the circumstances a pretty cool statement — the tactic was the same as Sir Richard Webster's in the House of Commons, contemptuous dismissal. In the event there were no "Noble Lords" ready with a question at hand. As the

Prime Minister had hinted, they accepted that so disgusting an affair was better passed over in gentlemanly silence. The House then turned to discussion of the Lunacy (Consolidation) Bill, a subject on which there was no shortage of speakers.

TEN

Averting a Royal
Scandal

The Prince of Wales had been laid up for much of the winter with an attack of bronchitis. He had not, however, been entirely inactive. It was known even before the debate in the House of Commons that Labouchere had been in contact with the Prince through his private secretary Sir Francis Knollys. One consequence of this contact was a story in *Truth* declaring that allegations in the foreign press about the Prince's attempts to hush up the affair were false. (*Truth* described his action throughout as "most laudable.) Another consequence was the information about the meeting between Lord Salisbury and Sir Dighton Probyn on October 18, 1889, at which the probability of Lord Arthur Somerset's arrest was discussed. The name on the scrap of paper which Labouchere offered the Attorney General and challenged him to read out in the Commons was Sir Francis Knollys. It is easy to see why Sir Richard Webster — suspecting that the source must have been a member of the royal household — brushed the offer aside and refused to read out the name. His Cleveland Street brief was difficult enough without going into the nightmarish ramifications of the royal connection.

Indeed, the more closely one examines the exchanges in the great debate the more striking is the intuitive skill of the Attorney General as a defender of the Establishment. Labouchere was scintillating in his presentation of a lost cause, but Sir Richard Webster was the better judge of the times and how to win. Ironically, it was the bruised Labouchere himself who gave one of the best tributes to the Attorney General's performance in a letter to *The Daily News* three days after the debate. He said of Sir Richard Webster:

He had a bad case. This was his misfortune, not his fault. I will do him full justice to say that he did his best with it. His "indignation" was perhaps a little too transparent; his praise of his profession was perhaps a little wearisome; but he perceived that his only chance was to fog the real issues, and this he did to the great satisfaction of the supporters of the Government, and with equal satisfaction to them he roundly abused the plaintiff. The jury that he addressed was a packed jury, their verdict was a foregone conclusion; for if my inferences had been admitted by them, and they had voted with me, there would have been a general election, and many of them would have lost their seats. Right may be all very well; but I can hardly blame them for acting on that first law of nature, self-preservation.

But Webster had done more than convince the "packed jury" of the Commons, he had effectively solidified the Establishment in its sense of outrage and created a moral climate in which any further references to Cleveland Street — there were very few — would be deemed a sign of social leprosy. *The Times* helped to further this process on the following day with a superbly constructed editorial which, as we can now see, was mistaken on almost every point of fact yet perfectly embodied the Establishment view. It began, as often happens on such occasions, with an invocation of the classics: "The old Latin maxim which prescribes concealment as well as punishment for certain kinds of offences emphatically holds good with regard to the scandals which Mr. Labouchere has deemed it his duty to force upon the public view." The writer conceded that if there was a well-founded case in which justice had been subordinated to concealment, an M.P. might be justified in raising such a topic. On the other hand, "his responsibility if he proceeds upon mere prurient gossip, stimulated by party malice, is grave indeed; and it is no less a responsibility than this which Mr Labouchere had unwisely incurred." The editorial then hinted at some kind of derangement in the faculties of the member for Northampton. "A preposterous suspicion with respect to the Prime Minister's supposed interference with the course of justice, in what is known as the Cleveland Street case, had somehow, or other taken deep root in his mind." There had been a time, the editorial noted sadly, when a Government obliged to defend itself against such "glaringly groundless charges" would have found warm support from the opposition front bench; regrettably party animosities had weakened and discredited such "healthy and honourable traditions of the House of Commons."

"Of the accusations themselves, after the comprehensive and conclusive answers of the Attorney-General, it is not necessary to say much." There was in Mr. Labouchere's presentation "a certain want of familiarity with the ordinary course of proceedings in our criminal courts, as well as with the provisions of the law of extradition" and it was very likely due to this deficiency that he fell victim to suspicions of which he would otherwise have recognized the "gross improbability." For Labouchere found on development of his theme that

It was not merely the Attorney-General or even the Home Secretary alone that he had been accusing but the Solicitor to the Treasury and its highly respected and irreproachable junior counsel [Mr. Avory], the newspaper press of the country, and last but not least, the Recorder of the City of London, who had been engaged in furthering the infamous design of those Ministerial officials. There was not one, in short, of Mr Labouchere's imputations which did not hit some one or other who is not only personally of high and unblemished repute, but is removed from any sort of temptation to commit corrupt or irregular acts. Every step forward multiplied the gross improbabilities which he had to surmount, and proved more and more clearly that the injurious aspersions against the Government — which have been refuted, and it is its sole redeeming feature, by the debate — might have been detected by him at the outset as so many baseless slanders.

Rarely, even in the somewhat specialized history of *Times* editorial writing, has so much credulous nonsense been stacked so high.

In reality the case against Lord Salisbury was much stronger than Labouchere realized or could probably have imagined. A potent illustration of this fact comes in one of the key documents that has recently become available in the Public Records Office. Despite the effortless dismissal of Labouchere's charges by *The Times*, nobody inside the Government who had any acquaintance with the case could be so carefree. On March 6, a week after the debate, Mr. W. H.

Smith, the First Lord of the Treasury who described the offense imputed by Labouchere as "worse than murder" and moved the motion for his suspension, asked the Hon. Hamilton Cuffe, the assistant director of Public Prosecutions, to prepare a memorandum analyzing the sources for Labouchere's speech. Cuffe, clearly suspecting an internal witch-hunt for the official or officials who "leaked" information to Labouchere, did the job with great diligence and care, producing a document of seventeen closely written pages with a five-page appendix. It is an intriguing document not the least because Cuffe clearly felt that he — or someone in the department — was among the suspects.

He had two sections in the appendix: "A" listed the facts and dates which Labouchere might have picked up from public sources, like the newspapers and court transcripts, and "B," considerably longer, listed the information which must have come from public servants on a confidential basis. Some of the information that Labouchere related to the House of Commons was new even to the DPP's department. Cuffe did not, for example, know the details of Mr. John Phillips's sleuthing work in Paris on behalf of the Post Office. "I had," Cuffe wrote, "no personal communication with any gentleman from the Post Office." But of the facts that were within Cuffe's knowledge, Labouchere had them all right with two minor exceptions — the date of the letter from the Foreign Office detailing Lord Salisbury's decision against application for Hammond's extradition from France was July 24, not July 25; the DPP's ruling against immediate application for Hammond's extradition from Belgium was on September 17, not September 16 as stated by Labouchere. Cuffe was evidently a little hurt by Labouchere's assertion that the Treasury had *ordered* the police to withdraw P.C. Hanks from attendance on Lord Arthur Somerset at his grandmother's funeral, but did not seriously quarrel with it. Cuffe stated that after receiving the Lord Chancellor's opinion, he was obliged to tell Commissioner Monro that he had no instructions to arrest: "My action — or inaction — was of course known to the Police and though I do not remember anything being said about the withdrawal of the Constable my inaction may have produced that result."

Cuffe noted that there were two matters of some significance that were known to some members of the DPP's department which were evidently not known by Labouchere. One was the fact that the case had been referred to the Lord Chancellor. The other was the general question of whether the papers on Lord Arthur Somerset should be sent to the War Office. But there was one much more significant fact of which *all* the members of the DPP's department were aware but which Labouchere did not know. Cuffe broached the point delicately in his memorandum:

Mr Labouchere praised the Police and included this Department in his censure and I think I am entitled to make the following observations.

His reasons for approving the conduct of the Police is that they did all they could to bring about the arrest of Hammond, and to institute proceedings against Lord Arthur Somerset — from his (Mr Labouchere's) point of view it strengthened his case that the Police would have instituted these proceedings had they not been prevented by the Treasury [*i.e.*, the Director of Public Prosecutions] and higher authorities — Taking this view — how much more would his case have been strengthened had he known that we in this Department advocated such proceedings — and refrained from action on express instructions — Sir A. Stephenson expressed his view in writing to the Home Office and the Attorney-General on several occasions and though his letters were kept confidential it was known to those here who had to do with the case that both he and I held the view that proceedings ought to be instituted.

At this point the document which survives in the Public Records Office — a departmental "flimsy" — becomes virtually indecipherable but Cuffe appears to be referring to an internal DPP memorandum, which (and here the writing becomes fully legible again) "from Mr. L's point of view it would be more important for him to know than I think anything he has mentioned. . . ." Presumably, from what we know of the DPP file on the case, Cuffe was referring to Sir Augustus Stephenson's long and bitter memorandum of September 15 (forwarded to the Attorney General on September 17) in which he disassociated his department from responsibility for conduct of the case.

The implication of Cuffe's memorandum was that if Labouchere had obtained all the information in the possession of the Treasury Solicitor he could have narrowed his charge of "conspiracy" to those above the level of the Director of Public Prosecutions, which would shorten his list of suspects to the Home Secretary, Henry Matthews; the Attorney General, Sir Richard Webster; the Lord Chancellor, Lord Halsbury; and the Prime Minister, Lord Salisbury.

Cuffe, however, was too careful a public servant to explicitly put this construction on the facts, though by hinting at this construction he effectively established that the DPP's department could not have been one of Labouchere's sources. Cuffe was clearly impressed by "how well on some points he [Labouchere] was informed by some one" but did not point the finger at any individual. He inferred that Labouchere's source, or more probably sources, worked in the police and/or Post Office departments. (If that were the case,

Labouchere's sources must have been at the highest level — probably Commissioner Monro and the Secretary to the Post Office.)

Cuffe drily concluded: "I have endeavoured to limit myself as far as possible to statements of fact which may be of assistance in any inquiry that may be made the issue of which it is not for me to prejudge." Cuffe's memorandum is the final document in the Public Records Office file on Cleveland Street. If there were an internal inquiry, no records of it have yet become available. It seems more likely that there was not. Cuffe's memorandum was almost certainly a sufficiently broad hint to his superiors that any inquiry was likely to prove more embarrassing to them than it would be to anyone found guilty of passing official secrets to Labouchere.

The central weakness of Labouchere's case against Lord Salisbury was a deficiency in his sources which, though good, were not nearly good enough. When it came down to it Labouchere could only draw the Prime Minister into the alleged role of conspirator on two occasions, once in July when he turned down the application for Hammond's extradition, and once in October when the equivocal interview with Sir Dighton Probyn took place. The importance of both occasions was deflected with comparative ease. The decision against extradition was conveyed, in the words of Sir Richard Webster, by "one of the official secretaries" at the Foreign Office "as a matter of routine business." The implication in the House of Commons was naturally that busy men like the Foreign Secretary and Prime Minister could not be expected to give every little detail of administration their personal attention. (Sir Richard naturally omitted the fact that the first line of the official's letter read: "The Marquess of Salisbury has given careful consideration. . . .") Lord Salisbury in the House of Lords was able to give a similar impression about the October meeting with Sir Dighton Probyn: "a casual interview . . . to which I did not attach the slightest importance. . . ." Again, the image of a busy man managing a world-wide empire, unable to give much attention to matters of small consequence like the Cleveland Street scandal.

It would have been impossible to sustain this image had all the facts in the Treasury Solicitor's file become public. From the documents that have become available, and it is scarcely likely that they contain a full record of all Lord Salisbury's activities in connection with the case, we can see that between those two "casual" events which Labouchere made public — the Attorney General (1) revised a firm opinion that Lord Arthur Somerset should be prosecuted in August after an interview with the Prime Minister; and (2) was eager to summons Lord Arthur in September but refrained from doing so because he did not have word from Lord Salisbury. Sir Richard Webster *knew*, whereas Labouchere only suspected, that every detail on the progress of the case was of absorbing interest to the Prime Minister. It is now possible to grasp more fully the dimensions of Sir Richard Webster's skill as a parliamentarian. Labouchere complimented him on adroit handling of a "bad" case, but it was better than that. The case was terrible.

The essential skill for a minister with a poor case to present to the Commons is the ability to mislead without actually lying. The House of Commons was (and is) a club, capable at times of profound cynicism, but one in which members felt a profound responsibility to one another. Back-benchers could accept being misled by ministers, especially when it was in their own interests. But a direct lie to the House of Commons, if found out, was never forgiven.

Labouchere touched on many of the sore points in the official handling of the Cleveland Street affair, and Sir Richard

Webster contrived to deal with them all, in a way that was totally misleading without ever telling a complete lie. The extent of the accomplishment on four main points is worth detailing:

1. To Labouchere's allegations that the pleas and light sentences in the Veck and Newlove trial had been a result of a deal between the defense and prosecution sanctioned by the authorities, Sir Richard replied "I wish to say that I neither directly nor indirectly made any arrangement with the prisoners' counsel as to what counts the prisoners should plead guilty to, and that there was no undertaking of any kind, either expressed or implied, as to what should be done by me or by the prisoners' counsel." Not a lie, perhaps, but a reply that represented less than a quarter truth. As we have seen, when Veck's counsel started plea-bargaining the whole question was referred to the Attorney General, and his reply by telegram was: "If both parties plead guilty do not proceed with charges of conspiracy unless counsel strongly advises." It was not perhaps an *instruction* to counsel to accept a plea to the more minor charges, but the chances of any counsel, retained by the DPP and acting under the authority of the Attorney General, "strongly advising" against such a course were virtually nil.

2. To Labouchere's allegation that the examination-in-chief of the post office boys before the magistrate was less than complete, Sir Richard asserted the complete impropriety of dragging in names "by a side wind . . . in order to elucidate a charge against another person." The Attorney General knew, of course, that Sir Augustus Stephenson, the DPP, originally considered that it was completely proper — indeed, necessary — that the examination of the boys should bring out the names of Lord Arthur Somerset and their other clients in Cleveland Street. It was only after a three-cornered debate

[196]

among himself, Sir Richard Webster, and the Home Secretary, that he agreed, against his better judgment, that the examination should elucidate "descriptions" of clients but not their real names. Sir Richard also knew that the magistrate, Mr. Hannay, only refrained from taking what he would have considered his normal course of dutiful action — elucidating the names of the boys' clients — because the case "concerned the Treasury."

3. To Labouchere's allegation that Lord Salisbury's refusal to apply for Hammond's extradition was not justified, Sir Richard asserted (a) that the refusal was "routine," and (b) that the extradition treaties with both France and Belgium did not cover Hammond's alleged offense. He gave no hint that the treaties were by no means clear on this point or that Mr. Horace Avory, the DPP's junior counsel, originally strongly disagreed with the Foreign Office's interpretation of the extradition treaties. Avory subsequently changed his mind, though both the Metropolitan Police and the Post Office remained convinced that an extradition application would be successful within the existing treaties.

4. To Labouchere's allegation that Lord Salisbury told Sir Dighton Probyn that a warrant for Lord Arthur Somerset's arrest was imminent, Sir Richard said, among other things, that this was not possible as he did not personally decide to make application for a warrant against Lord Arthur until two weeks after the Prime Minister's meeting with the Prince's representative. Again, this was technically true but totally misleading. Although the warrant for Lord Arthur Somerset's arrest was not applied for until the second week in November, *all* the evidence to buttress the application was in the Attorney General's hands by the first week in September. In a strictly legal sense the evidence for Lord Arthur Somerset's imminent arrest was not only available at the time of

[197]

Lord Salisbury's meeting with Sir Dighton Probyn but had been available for no less than six weeks before that meeting. There was nothing after the meeting, except perhaps the revival of the Attorney General's sense of moral purpose, that made the case for Lord Arthur Somerset's arrest any stronger. Indeed, it actually became marginally weaker. When the decision to apply for a warrant was made, the DPP's office found that it had mislaid the three twenty-shilling postal orders which Algernon Allies said had been sent to him by his aristocratic lover. They were subsequently found, but because of their temporary loss the information on which the arrest warrant was based made no mention of their existence.

Sir Richard showed one other talent for ministerial obfuscation that only the most skilled parliamentarians can get away with. The stratagem might be described as the shrewd confession of weakness. He admitted to the Commons that he did not "altogether trust" his own judgment in the matter, taking the House into his confidence about his consultations with the Lord Chancellor. Nothing could appear more convincing; here was an eminent legal authority confessing that on some cases his concern for the individual was so great that he felt he had to defer to a still greater eminence. The fact that it was no part of the Lord Chancellor's job to waste his time on consideration of a case involving a misdemeanor could be forgiven by such a humble disclosure. Backbenchers were evidently charmed by this confession of noninfallibility in a Minister, and what seemed to be a frank revelation of background of which even the accuser Labouchere was unaware.

However, a truly frank revelation of background should have included the fact that the Attorney General himself was in early August in favor of prosecuting Lord Arthur Somerset even before the powerful corroborating evidence of

Algernon Allies came into his possession; that in late August the Director of Public Prosecutions argued that the evidence against Lord Arthur was "stronger than that against Veck" who had already been charged; and that the same Director who, unlike the Lord Chancellor, had contact with all the potential witnesses and a day-to-day experience of prosecution, had informed the Attorney General in mid-September of his complete disagreement with the way the case was being handled. What the Minister frankly did not say in the Commons was a good deal more important than what he frankly did say.

As it was, Sir Richard Webster contrived the impression that there was no disagreement on the part of the authorities, merely a long and diligent search for the correct course of action which, as luck would have it, was only completed after Lord Arthur Somerset had fled the country. That Sir Richard Webster was able to win such a case and engineer the suspension of the plaintiff without uttering a total falsehood about the facts was a remarkable achievement even before the "packed jury" of a Tory-dominated House of Commons. As far as we are able to establish, Sir Richard told only one 24-carat lie, and this was not in response to Labouchere but in reply to a needling question by Charles Bradlaugh, the junior Radical M.P. for Northampton, who found it hard to understand why the Attorney General had consulted with the Lord Chancellor on three occasions; could this conceivably be explained by the social position of the suspect? Hansard does not give any inkling of the straightness or otherwise of the Attorney General's face in making the reply: "I made no distinction whatever in respect of the persons."

Was there a criminal conspiracy? Labouchere's charge still requires some kind of answer, perhaps the more so now we can appreciate that the facts on which he based it were more substantial than even he suspected. The assessment is hard to make, partly because ideas of what constitutes conspiracy vary so widely. The late nineteenth-century Tories were, for example, fond of accusing the Irish members of the House of employing criminally conspiratorial methods. Such charges naturally became so much sentimental debating rhetoric in the cooler climate of the twentieth century when Ireland (at least all but six counties) achieved its freedom.

There is, of course, no dispute that the ends of justice were defeated in the case of Lord Arthur Somerset, but it was certainly not true that all the parties who helped this outcome were consciously working with that end in mind. In the final analysis, even the hapless Sir Richard Webster was the reverse of cynical cover-up artist. The picture of him that emerges from the private files of the case is of a tortured man who always wants to do his duty but can never be quite sure what it is. Had someone approached him immediately after Lord Arthur Somerset came under suspicion with a nineteenth-century version of "OK, A.G., fix it so he beats the rap and gets us off the hook," one can imagine Sir Richard striking the blackguard with a muscular Christian fist.

What Labouchere was up against was something much more complex than a straightforward conspiracy. Essentially, he was confronting an Establishment prepared to suspend some of its normal judgments in response to a higher duty. Once the impulse passed through it that Lord Salisbury, the Prime Minister, was not keen on charges being pressed, everyone concerned started acting slightly out of character.

No one individual totally compromised his principles, but a whole host of characters receiving this impulse, either directly or at a remove, pushed them to the limit. We can now see clearly the progression of this impulse down from Henry

[200]

Matthews, Home Secretary and head of a great department of state, to the humble P.C. 298 "Jack" Sladden bashing his beat in the Tottenham Court Road. Matthews, presumably in deference to Lord Salisbury's wishes, held out until the middle of September against the Attorney General's wavering view that Lord Arthur Somerset should be prosecuted. The Attorney General, anxious to please his political superiors and do his duty, of which the Director of Public Prosecutions provided constant and uncomfortable reminders, prevaricated until November but he finally did what he intended to do in the first place — preferred charges against Lord Arthur Somerset. The DPP compromised his original attitude to the case to the extent of ensuring that the evidence-in-chief of the boys did not elicit Lord Arthur Somerset's name in open court, but he then put firmly on record his disgust at the whole proceeding and, from the middle of September, disclaimed all responsibility for conduct of the case. Mr. Horace Avory, the junior counsel retained by the DPP, initially saw no obstacle to Hammond's extradition but later changed his mind. Mr. Hannay, the magistrate involved in the Veck and Newlove hearing, compromised his principles to the extent of not asking the boys the names of their clients. His conscience was eased by informing the DPP that he wanted the Attorney General to know of this compromise. The Metropolitan Police and the Post Office eased their sense of bureaucratic guilt by leaking details of what they knew to the press and Labouchere. But at the very base of the official pyramid, where P.C. Sladden moved and had his being, the contradictions must have seemed intolerable. After months on stakeout duty, in close acquaintance with the post office boys, his conviction of Lord Arthur Somerset's guilt must have been total, yet there was no apparent action by his superiors. Small wonder that at the end of the day his sense of duty was sufficiently eroded for him to try and act as a go-between for Lord Arthur Somerset's solicitor, Arthur Newton, and the boys who had the evidence that could put Lord Arthur in jail.

It seems unlikely (though not all the evidence is in) that Lord Salisbury and P.C. 298 Sladden personally conspired together; at the same time there is no question that they both ultimately served an end that effectively perverted the course of justice in the Cleveland Street affair.

The real question is why Lord Salisbury transmitted his subtly corrupting message through the bureaucracy in the first place. There is nothing in the public or private records of the case to suggest that he had any special connection with Lord Arthur Somerset, much less that he had any particular sympathy for homosexuals. It is very likely true that, if he gave the matter much thought, he would rather Lord Arthur Somerset had not been so stupid as to be caught, particularly at a time when his (Lord Salisbury's) own brother-in-law, the Earl of Galloway, was exciting comment as an alleged child-molester. (Lord Galloway was in October 1889 eventually found "not guilty" of molesting a ten-year-old girl in Dumfries; in January 1890 he was charged with molesting a sixteen-year-old girl in Glasgow and was again acquitted.) Lord Salisbury, however, was not, by all accounts, a very sentimental man, and the nineteenth century was littered with the yellowing bones of aristocrats who had been publicly disgraced in one way or another. Those members of Society who broke the eleventh commandment, "Thou shalt not be found out," were normally consigned to oblivion without undue heartaches by former friends. Lord Salisbury could have borne Lord Arthur Somerset's conviction for a homosexual crime with great fortitude, unless there were considerations other than personal involved.

The only conceivable explanation of Lord Salisbury's conduct throughout the affair is that it was guided by reasons of state. It was not necessary that he should either believe or disbelieve the rumors about Prince Eddy's homosexual proclivities, but the prospect of his name being mentioned in a homosexual scandal was enough to cause alarm. Prince Eddy was only two deaths from the Crown, and neither in the year 1889 seemed terribly remote. The Queen was old and the Prince of Wales had once been almost mortally ill and indulged appetites in a way that was not normally conducive to longevity. The prospect of maintaining the ideology of Empire — based more on subtle ties of loyalty, sentiment, and trade than on force — around the person of an undistinguished young man who was publicly tainted with homosexual tendencies must have been appalling.

It is possible to make out a prima facie case of criminal conspiracy, but it is not quite the case that Labouchere presented in the House of Commons. For a conspiracy charge to be effective, it is necessary to establish that the principals deliberately desired an outcome at variance with the requirements of justice. The record shows that there were only two men who were deliberately, consistently, and without apparent reservation set on a course that would prevent Lord Arthur Somerset coming to trial and they happened to be the Prime Minister and the Prince of Wales. (Some circumstantial evidence suggests that the Lord Chancellor might be drawn in as an accessory.)

The prime mover in this conspiracy was, of course, not the Prime Minister but the Prince of Wales, who had both personal affection for Lord Arthur Somerset and, more importantly, the desire to deflect any suspicion from his own son as reasons for seeing the Cleveland Street affair laid decently to rest. Labouchere might be flattered by the Prince of Wales's assertion that he was the only man in the kingdom to treat him as a social equal, but when it came down to it Labouchere was as impressed by majesty as the next man. He accepted and publicized the line — both in *Truth* and the House of Commons — about the Prince of Wales being on the side of full publicity and justice for the miscreants. Nothing could more completely free the monarchy from damaging rumors than the endorsement of Labouchere — a tireless radical and republican and rigorous critic of the royal finances. When Labouchere said his piece in the House of Commons about a certain "eminent gentleman" (the Prince of Wales) using all his efforts to publicize the case, the M.P.s may have thought that he was dispelling extraneous gossip in order to identify the real villain — Lord Salisbury. In fact, he was the unwitting accomplice in the last act of the cover-up. He ended the work that Lord Salisbury had begun — ensuring that the royal family was placed entirely above suspicion.

Perhaps the central fascination of the Cleveland Street affair is the evidence it provides of conflict between various concepts of duty. The Victorians, whatever their other blind spots, had very high standards of civic morality. For the middle classes the idea of doing other than one's duty required a stupendous leap of the imagination. Cleveland Street cut through concepts of public duty in a terrifying way. It was the duty of the Post Office, if only out of respect for the Queen's uniform, to ensure that their young employees were not debauched. It was the duty of the police to bring the criminals, whoever they might be, to justice. It was the duty of the Treasury Solicitor acting as Director of Public Prosecutions to ensure that justice was done speedily and seen to be done. It was the duty of the Home Secretary and Attorney General to ensure that the police and public prosecutors did their jobs honestly and effectively. It was the duty of the Prime Minister to maintain Her Majesty's government, uphold her laws, and ensure the continuity of the realm under her possible successors. There was, however, no way in which all these codes of duty could be properly discharged at the same time.

It required an act of ultimate cynicism or statesmanship, depending on one's point of view, that would allow all these great public figures and departments of state to feel that they had discharged their obligations and yet avert the most damaging potential consequences of the scandal. The Prince of Wales provided the only way out of the labyrinth by, on the one hand, implying to Lord Salisbury that the best solution was to ensure that Lord Arthur Somerset conveniently escape justice and never darken the doors of England again, and, on the other, by convincing Labouchere that he like every honest citizen was in favor of full disclosure and the full rigor of the law in such cases. Never was a royal bet better hedged.

It is hard to feel anything other than admiration for the Prince of Wales's duplicity. By this stage in his life he was something of an adept at what might be called the art of royal scandal-management, and his interest was not the myth of monarchy but monarchy itself. To paraphrase Labouchere in another context, right may not have been on his side but we can hardly blame him for acting on that first law of nature, self-preservation.

While the Prince of Wales was accomplishing the amazing feat of reducing the most dangerous Victorian scandal to the level of the least significant, Prince Eddy was kept busy in India. But the "problem of Eddy," like that of the Prince of Wales himself thirty years earlier, was heavy on the minds of the royal family. The solution again was thought to be marriage.

On 19 March 1890, the Prince of Wales departed for Berlin to take up the offer of a state visit made by Kaiser Wilhelm. He carried in his pocket a list, compiled by Queen Victoria, of possible princesses for his eldest son to marry. At the head of the list was the Kaiser's younger sister, Princess Margaret (Mossy). As it turned out "Mossy" was not frightfully keen on the prospect of life with Britain's strange Heir Presumptive. Still, the Prince of Wales had a very pleasant visit to Germany. He wrote to Queen Victoria, shortly before leaving Berlin for the South of France: "When you next write to him [the Kaiser] please thank him, as he treated me quite like a Sovereign and considered my visit as in your name — in fact, as your representative; and I am very sorry to say that my expenses, in consequence, have been heavy." On March 30, the *Reynolds's Newspaper* Court reporter recorded: "Prince Albert Victor is still sporting himself in his own way in India. On Wednesday he laid the foundation stone of a Leper Asylum in Bombay." Life for the royal family had returned to normal.

ELEVEN

Death of the Young Prince

On Tuesday, 20 May 1890, the last public act of the Cleveland Street drama was played out before Mr. Justice Cave in the Queen's Bench division. The scene was the sentencing of Mr. Arthur Newton, Lord Arthur Somerset's solicitor, who had pleaded guilty to a charge of perverting the course of justice. By then the event was of scant public interest; the fireworks were over and the guilty plea threatened to turn the proceedings into a formality. Mr. Justice Cave, with marked exasperation, detected that someone was trying to use him to preside over a charade.

This sequel to Scotland Yard's crusading efforts to incriminate Newton and his two assistants, Henry Taylerson and Augustus De Gallo, showed a surprising lack of fervor. The charge against De Gallo, who was most directly concerned in the attempt to transport the potentially damaging witnesses among the post office boys to Australia, had already been dropped, possibly because P.C. Sladden had been a link-man in this impertinent enterprise. However, both Newton and Taylerson had been indicted on six counts, covering the attempts to persuade Algernon Allies and the post office boys to leave the country, the squaring of Charles Hammond, and other minor services to the cause of Lord Arthur's escape from justice.

The hearing of the evidence had been completed in one day on the previous Friday (May 16). Sir Charles Russell had led for the defense, while the prosecution, if that is the word to describe the kid-glove approach to the defendants, had been conducted by Sir Richard Webster, still the Attorney General, and still instinctively adept at killing potentially dangerous situations with ostensible kindness.

Newton's committal hearing had heard harsh words about the authorities. His counsel implied that the inexperienced Newton, on the bottom-most rung of the legal hierarchy, could scarcely be blamed when the highest authority in the land had been so manifestly unwilling to bring Lord Arthur Somerset to trial. But the trial had revealed Sir Charles Russell at his emollient best. His client had decided, on reflection, that while he must plead not guilty to the five *specific* counts in the indictment, he would plead guilty to the general charge of "perverting the course of justice." Russell described his client Newton as a victim of his own zeal and the desire to protect his clients from blackmail; he understood that "two or three" of his clients (among them, of course, Lord Arthur Somerset) had been endangered by the Cleveland Street raid. They had assured Newton that attempts had been made to blackmail them. As for Henry Taylerson, he had acted under Newton's instructions at all times, and therefore pleaded not guilty on all counts.

[208]

The Attorney General had apparently appreciated Taylerson's subordinate role; and offered no evidence against him. His plea was accepted without comment. The Attorney General also displayed extreme sympathy for Newton himself. It was a case of a young man being carried away by enthusiasm. While not being able to endorse all the arguments of the defending counsel, Sir Richard did feel that the facts were consistent with Newton's affirmation of excess zeal and the desire to defend his clients from blackmail. The jury obediently accepted Newton's plea of not guilty on the specific counts. Mr. Justice Cave, who had listened to this forensic love-in with mounting impatience, was now left with nothing more demanding to do than sentence Newton.

With due respect to both eminent counsel, Mr. Justice Cave was "sorry to say" that he did not accept their opinion. Newton's extreme youth might be an argument in mitigation, but he could not share the view that the desire to defend his clients from blackmail was a motivating factor. He, therefore, did not feel that a fine would be appropriate as this would in all probability be paid by the wealthy clients who had encouraged Newton's improper activities in the first place. He then sentenced Newton to six weeks' imprisonment. It was, under the circumstances, a modest penalty, though perhaps somewhat harsher than Newton had hoped after his first day in court. No suggestion of a quid pro quo survives in the records, but Newton went off to prison meekly enough, without ever making good the boast which had virtually paralyzed the higher authorities eight months earlier. He refrained from dragging the name of Prince Albert Victor into the affair.

Prince Eddy, having completed his comprehensive tour of the Indian Empire, taking in Egypt, Greece, and France en route home, arrived back in London just as Newton was going to jail. It was a measure of the success of the cover-up that nobody, by this time, could conceive of any connection between the two events. The Prince was created Duke of Clarence and Avondale on 24 May 1890, Queen Victoria's seventy-first birthday. The gesture was meant to reflect honor on his position as Heir Presumptive rather than as a reward for his personal achievements.

Stripped of the accretion of myth which has attached itself so persistently to his character, he can be seen at this stage in his career as a poignant and even persecuted figure. His exaggerated dressiness, which had earned him the "Collar and Cuffs" nickname, was an inheritance from his sartorially splendid father. The high collars also served another purpose. Like his mother Alexandra, Eddy suffered from deafness and as an adolescent had fallen into the habit of tilting his head to one side — it didn't mean he was an idiot, but simply that he was perpetually craning to try to catch something that had escaped him. The high collars had been devised to keep that royal head impeccably straight; and so for him were a discomfort, not unlike the backboards which other Victorian child-torturers had invented "to teach posture." Eddy, again like Alexandra, had a scar on his throat, the result of a minor operation — his collars thus served a cosmetic purpose as well. Appearance was the essence of his life; his regiment, the Tenth Hussars, could boast no less a figure than Beau Brummel among its former officers. But for the Prince the price was more or less permanent constraint.

Such glimpses of Eddy "off duty" that have survived give an impression not of a monster but of a mild and even gentle personality. His correspondence to his old Cambridge friends — one of them, Harry Wilson, was constantly sending him appalling occasional verses — are models of thoughtfulness; he would make time to fit in a dinner and was always ready to send a signed photograph as a souvenir for a relation. The same is true of his letters to his former tutor J. K. Stephen which, though affectionate and friendly, contain no suggestion of a homosexual attachment between the two. Eddy was also far from sharing Stephen's obsessive hate of women; just the reverse, his letters are full of references to attractive women by whom he had been favorably impressed. Nonetheless, there are yawning gaps in the biographical material that can be found; his sinister reputation, including the theory that he was Jack the Ripper, has emerged more from the omissions than from any evidence that has survived.

Marrying him off became a family obsession and one that presented many difficulties. He refused to even consider the Prussian Princess Margaret ("Mossy") who had never shown any enthusiasm for him. Now Princess Alix of Hesse ("Alicky"), her eyes set on the timid Nicholas, Tsarevitch of Russia, rejected him. (She achieved her ambition and became the last Empress of Russia, only to perish with "Nicky" and the five children at Ekaterinburg in July 1918.) Contrary as ever, Eddy fell in love with Princess Hélène d'Orléans, daughter of the Comte de Paris, the Pretender to the French throne. The Queen had specifically warned him against such a match, since Hélène, like all the Bourbons, was naturally a Roman Catholic. But the sentimental side of the Queen's character, increasingly noticeable in old age, spurred her to a reluctant blessing after the couple became engaged at the end of August 1890, while staying at Mar Lodge in Scotland with the Duke of Fife. Princess Hélène's masculinity — she smoked a pipe while deerstalking, and the Prince of Wales's cigars after dinner — raised some courtly eyebrows, but the true impediment to the match was the religious one. English monarchs had to swear, among other things, an intention to Defend the (Protestant) Faith. "What the ultimate result may be, God only knows," wrote the Prince to his younger son George, two months after the engagement; "I am not very sanguine." He discussed the question with President Carnot of France while passing through Paris in October 1890 but the *mésalliance* refused to sort itself out — despite Princess Hélène's intrepid attempts to persuade both her father and the Pope that a way round could be found, and her willingness to renounce the Roman Catholic faith.

The Prince of Wales's pessimism deepened as the year closed and it became clear this marriage was an impossibility. His biographer, Sir Philip Magnus, normally so reticent, describes the Prince's dilemma in the following terms:

He braced himself to face resolutely the problem posed by his elder son. He decided to persuade the Princess [Alexandra], if he could, that the Duke of Clarence, whose dissipated life was beginning to cause scandal, must either marry suitably during 1891, or be despatched on a tour of South Africa, Australia and New Zealand, as a punishment and to preserve him from harm.

The blighted courtship of Princess Hélène was abandoned shortly thereafter but "the problem of Eddy" declined to go away. No less than three different plans were devised for him in the summer of 1891; what they had in common was keeping him away from London. "By now," Magnus writes, his parents "were almost at their wits end to know what to do. . . . The Princess of Wales wanted the Duke to remain in Ireland with his regiment (the Tenth Hussars), so she could control and see him as much as possible; Queen Victoria wanted him to travel in Europe; and the Prince of Wales wanted to send him, as a punishment and precaution, to the farthest ends of the Empire."

The Queen, possibly because she was kept in ignorance, showed more indulgence towards her erring grandson than his parents, who knew him better. Her feeling was that his education, despite the early world tour and his Indian visit, had made him too insular. The Prince of Wales, now convinced that Eddy must be removed from the army as soon as possible, wrote her an unusually candid letter on the subject on August 5, 1891. "If you think Eddy too English it is a good fault in these days and will make him much more popular. . . . His education and future have been a matter of some considerable anxiety to us, and the difficulty of rousing him is very great. A good sensible wife with some considerable character is what he needs most, but where is she to be found?"

Where indeed? Eddy's reputation had traveled ahead of him, so much so that Europe's eligible families were showing a marked reluctance to offer their daughters, even when the not inconsiderable bait of the throne of England was dangled before them. Queen Victoria found it hard to comprehend; she was convinced that a tour of European courts would somehow brighten Eddy up. Sir Francis Knollys wrote a characteristically firm note on the subject to the Prime Minister's private secretary, again in August 1891 when concern for Eddy's future reached its peak:

As you are aware, the Queen strongly advocates Prince Eddy travelling in Europe, instead of visiting the Cape of Good Hope (or, rather, South Africa), New Zealand, Canada, etc. Unfortunately her views on *certain social* subjects [Knolly's italics] are so strong, that the Prince of Wales does not like to tell her his real reason for sending Prince Eddy away, which is intended as a *punishment*, and as a means of keeping him out of harm's way; and I am afraid that neither of those objects would be attained by his simply travelling about Europe. She is therefore giving her advice in the dark.

The matter was argued over throughout the month and in the end Princess Alexandra's views prevailed, a tribute to her stubbornness. Eddy was to be left with his regiment for the winter. Meanwhile a plan had been devised to marry him off to Princess Victoria Mary ("May") of Teck, a family cousin who had been brought up in England, was twenty-three years old and extremely poor. Even so, there were doubts about how amenable the girl would prove.

Knollys, who was beginning to look like a marriage broker, wrote to Sir Henry Ponsonby, the Queen's private secretary, discussing the scheme with a certain caution, again in August 1891: "I think the preliminaries are now pretty well settled, but do you suppose Princess May will make any resistance? I do not anticipate any real opposition on Prince Eddy's part if he is properly managed and is told he *must* do it — that it is for the good of the country, etc., etc."

Knollys's qualified optimism was justified; the proposal was made and accepted on December 3, 1891: the country and the empire, who knew little about the postulant bridegroom except that he was Heir Presumptive and had acquired the "Collar and Cuffs" nickname, gave themselves over to some mild and sentimental pleasure at the prospect of an important royal wedding. A formidable collection of assorted royalty was gathering at Sandringham at the beginning of the new year to celebrate Eddy's twenty-eighth birthday, which was also intended as an engagement party — the wedding was scheduled for March or April. On January 7, the eve of his birthday, Eddy was taken ill while attending a local shooting party. He left his bed the following day for a few hours to receive his birthday presents but soon retired again. He was suffering from influenza, which reached epidemic proportions in Europe that winter; in due course it turned into pneumonia, before which the specialists were helpless. He died six days later, which meant his younger brother George became Heir Presumptive. Magnus describes this development as "a merciful act of providence."

·⊰{ TWELVE }⊱·

Destroying the Evidence

The Cleveland Street affair, though short in time-span —
less than eight months had elapsed between its first ten-
tative mention in the press and the damp-squib trial of Arthur
Newton that was its public epilogue — affected many lives at
many levels. In some cases the wounds inflicted by the affair
never healed; whereas others survived not only unscathed but
with greatly enhanced careers. The subsequent history of the
main characters indicates that the suppressors of truth fared
rather better than the apostles of disclosure. The official architects of the cover-up all prospered.

LORD SALISBURY continued on his patrician way. His party
narrowly lost the election in 1892, and W. E. Gladstone came
back for his fourth term as Prime Minister, bent on giving
home rule to Ireland. But the Irish question split Gladstone's

party so fundamentally that Salisbury made an effortless comeback in 1895 with a massively increased majority.

Eventually he managed to bring an additional one hundred million new subjects under the aegis of the British crown, while giving the impression that he would rather have been at Hatfield conducting some scholarly experiments in the physical sciences. Like the aging Bismarck, whom he replaced as arbiter of Europe, he was as attracted by consolidation and security as he was repelled by sabre-rattling and melodrama. Queen Victoria regarded him, in an age that included her beloved Disraeli as well as Gladstone, as her most outstanding prime minister. Had she said this to his face he would no doubt have switched the topic of conversation.

His policy on the partition of Africa was motivated more by a desire to preempt the Germans and French than by any intrinsic urge for aggrandizement. He was shocked by the upstart Cecil Rhodes, who when asked by Queen Victoria how he had been occupying his time, replied, "Enlarging Your Majesty's Empire, ma'am."

There were disappointments of course. The Boer War in South Africa had frayed the myth of British invincibility, but Salisbury had already prepared the way for a more modest policy of European alliances. He was to be the prime minister who saw the new century in, and after the death of Queen Victoria scarcely needed to remind the new King, Edward VII, that the monarchy was in his debt as a result of his role in the Cleveland Street affair.

Having secured a suitable settlement to the Boer problem, Salisbury retired from public life in July 1902, pausing only to ensure that his nephew, A. J. Balfour, was invited by Edward VII to continue the family tradition of leadership. The

King thought Balfour too waspish by half and cried "Nepotism" — a pleasantry the Marquess accepted deadpan, content that he had got what he wanted. It had almost become a habit. He died a year later on August 22, 1903.

LORD HALSBURY, the Lord Chancellor, survived the Cleveland Street affair in the style to which he had become accustomed. He completed his enormous and definitive work, *Halsbury's Laws of England,* that is still on every law student's book list and, in 1895, was again appointed Lord Chancellor after the brief Liberal interregnum. When he retired in 1905 he had held this office for no less than seventeen years. He died in 1921.

HENRY MATTHEWS, the Home Secretary, was gently eased out of the firing line in 1895 when he was elevated to the House of Lords and took the title of Viscount Llanduff. There he remained, in contented obscurity, until his death in 1913, aged eighty-seven.

SIR RICHARD WEBSTER was reappointed Attorney General in 1895 when Salisbury was returned to power, and held the post for five more years, when he became Master of the Rolls and a Privy Counsellor, both highly dignified posts. In 1914, he published a book, *Recollections of Bar and Bench,* which is described under his entry in the Dictionary of National Biography as "badly written and not very interesting." It gave nothing away; Cleveland Street was not mentioned. He died the following year.

SIR DIGHTON PROBYN, whose brief exchanges with Lord Salisbury at King's Cross station were so helpful to Lord Arthur and the Prince of Wales, grew old and even more honored in the service of the Crown. He became Keeper of the Privy Purse, a suitable post for a man of his discretion, when Edward became King, and after his master's death he was appointed Comptroller for Dowager Queen Alexandra's household.

Despite persistent rumors that "an understanding" existed between him and the Hon. Charlotte Knollys, Sir Francis (later Lord) Knollys's sister, they both died unmarried — he in June 1924, she in April 1930. His decorations mounted up as the years passed; his ultimate style was Field Marshall the Rt. Hon. Sir Dighton Probyn, V.C., G.C.B., G.C.S.I., G.C.V.O.

SIR FRANCIS KNOLLYS, the Prince's private secretary, was made a baron in 1902, shortly after his master succeeded to the throne, and continued in the same position, serving as joint private secretary to George V after his master died in 1910, until retiring in February 1914. He played a crucial and controversial part in the House of Lords' constitutional crises of 1910; in 1913 he wrote to King George explaining there was one more task he had to perform before making way for a younger man.

It is necessary, however, that I should first look over, sort and, *when advisable, destroy* [our italics] the great mass of letters and papers of all descriptions which accumulated at Marlborough House, and which have since accumulated at Buckingham Palace — in fact from the year 1863 to the present day.

King Edward's will had already specified that his entire private and personal correspondence, "including especially those with Queen Alexandra and with Queen Victoria," should be destroyed. Knollys helped Lord Esher (formerly Reginald Brett), who had previously edited Queen Victoria's letters for publication; between them they turned the process of censorship into a veritable holocaust.

Together with Esher, who had destroyed all the private letters between Disraeli and both Queen Victoria and the Prince of Wales, as well as "a mass of material relating to George IV in the royal archives" at Windsor, Knollys could claim to have done more than anyone to obliterate the traces which posterity might have used to answer innumerable important (and not always simply indiscreet) royal questions. Between them the two courtiers got rid of many more documents than even Princess Beatrice, who destroyed, without transcribing, major portions of the diary Queen Victoria had kept up since she was a girl in the 1830s. It is impossible to assess which of them did posterity more harm since, as Sir Philip Magnus says, the loss is "irreparable and incalculable."

Lord Knollys, G.C.B., G.C.V.O., K.C.M.G., I.S.O., died, aged eighty-seven, in August 1924, with a clear conscience. To the very end he had faithfully occupied himself obliterating his master's traces "where he thought advisable."

Those whose actions were only of incidental — but still valuable — use to the Establishment when it came to getting the scandal settled, also found their later careers prospered. LORD EUSTON found that his public admission to an interest in *poses plastiques* closed no doors in Society. He became ever more prominent in masonic circles and was appointed Grand Master of the "Mark Masons." King Edward VII showed him special consideration by appointing him an A.D.C. in his coronation year. However, his lordship never succeeded to the Grafton dukedom. He died of dropsy in 1912 while his father was still alive.

SIR CHARLES RUSSELL, who had represented both Lord Euston and Arthur Newton so ably in the courtroom, was rapidly promoted. In 1894 he was appointed Lord Chief Justice and elevated to the peerage as Lord Russell of Killowen — he was the first Roman Catholic to become the Lord Chief Justice since the Reformation.

CHARLES HAMMOND, the conveniently fugitive proprietor of 19 Cleveland Street, arrived safely in Seattle from which haven he gave, in March 1890, a brief interview that was carried in the mass-circulation *Reynolds's Newspaper*. He paradoxically threatened to reveal all but also denied that he had anything to do with the seamy side of Cleveland Street. He insisted that the authorities had confused two different houses in Cleveland Street, an attitude which implied he had lost none of his old-fashioned panache in the New World. *The New York Herald* published an unconfirmed story in 1893 claiming he had bought what was described as "a tract of land and a hotel" in Ellensburg, Washington state. All trace of him was lost to historians when the census returns for 1900 were destroyed by fire in 1936.

ARTHUR NEWTON survived the Cleveland Street episode with his customary bounce. The wound inflicted on his reputation by his six weeks in jail healed rapidly, leaving only the faintest trace of scar tissue. The consensus in the legal profession seemed to be that he had done sufficient penance for his youthful indiscretion and the question of whether he should be struck off — debarred from the practice of law — did not apparently arise. He resumed his practice in Marlborough Street on coming out of prison and went on to become one of London's most famous solicitors, specializing in crime and *causes célèbres*. Mr. Justice Cave, however, was a better judge of Arthur Newton's potential than the other legal experts involved in his trial. Where they saw an impetuous young man in a hurry, Cave had spotted a devious crook in embryo.

Twenty years later, Newton again achieved public notoriety as the solicitor representing Dr. Peter Crippen, the American doctor who made history by becoming the first murderer to be identified on the high seas after the captain of the vessel had used the new-fangled instrument the radio to communicate his suspicions to Scotland Yard. When the S.S. *Montrose* docked in Quebec, he and his companion, Miss Ethel Le Neve, who was disguised as a boy, were arrested and taken back to London. The case attracted great public attention and although Dr. Crippen maintained his innocence of the crime of murdering his wife, the evidence against him was overwhelming. The police had discovered the incomplete remains of Mrs. Crippen, who had called herself "Belle Elmore," at their London home in Hilldrop Crescent, and found traces of the poison, hyoscine. They had also traced the chemist who had sold five grains of this substance to Dr. Crippen shortly before his wife disappeared. Arthur Newton clearly did his best to get his client acquitted (Miss Le Neve was acquitted of being an accessory), but Crippen was duly found guilty and sentenced to death. On the day after the hanging, Newton completed the sale of Dr. Crippen's death-cell "confession" to Horatio Bottomley, who gave the story maximum prominence in his sensational magazine *John Bull*. The Law Society was not amused.

For one thing Crippen had made no eve-of-the-gallows confession; for another, the Law Society disapproved of a solicitor breaching a client's confidence — real or imaginary — on the day of his execution. This recurrence of Newton's "impetuosity" in middle life earned him a twelve-month suspension from practice (July 1911 to July 1912).

A year after his suspension expired Newton was back at the Old Bailey in yet more spectacular circumstances. This time, however, he occupied the center of the stage in a trial involving himself. He was accused of conspiracy to defraud and of obtaining £13,500 in money and securities by false pretenses. Apart from Newton it involved three other main characters: William Henry (alias "Berkeley Barnard") Bennett, his codefendant in the dock and a veteran of two personal bankruptcies, from the last of which he was still undischarged; Mr. Hans Thorsch, a young Austrian gentleman who had come into a large inheritance from which, so it emerged, the defendants had tried to separate him; and Count Andor Festetics, a Hungarian speculator and gambler, whose range of self-proclaimed accomplishments included a win in the Hungarian Grand National and fencing victories over the six finest swordsmen in Europe. The gay ghost of the Count hovered over the Old Bailey proceedings but the corporeal Festetics had long since departed the scene; he had no desire to cross his immaculate blade with the cudgel of the men from Scotland Yard.

Of the £13,500 paid out by Thorsch, Newton had £4,000 and Festetics had £4,000 for their own private use, while a mere £3,915 had been sent to Canada to pay retroactively for forest land they had sold to Thorsch but did not actually own at the time of sale. Bennett's share of the proceeds in this remarkable transaction was £1,585.

The trial at the Old Bailey lasted five days; Newton struck many attitudes of injured innocence, and conducted his own defense. Nonetheless, on 23 July 1913, the jury required less than half an hour to find both defendants guilty. Newton who had once before, within living memory of the courts, managed to minimize the consequences of his illegal acts by pleading in mitigation the hot-blooded intemperateness of youth, now tried to melt the judge's heart by drawing attention to the decrepitude of his late middle age.

Newton told Mr. Justice Ridley that he was fifty-three years of age and suffering from a very painful internal complaint — catarrh of the stomach. He stood there an absolutely ruined man. He had nothing whatever in the world to go on with — no means or resources of any kind. He hoped that the judge would give him another chance.

The judge, however, was more impressed by the "gross scheme of fraud" than by Newton's personal predicament. He sentenced Newton to three years' penal servitude, and Bennett to eighteen months' imprisonment with hard labor. Newton was formally struck off by the Law Society and never practiced law again, but he was a resilient man and his health stood up well to the prison ordeal. He lived on for fourteen years after his release, dying in 1930 at a fashionable address in Ebury Street, two hundred yards from Buckingham Palace.

There is no record of whether Newton kept up his acquaintance with Algernon Allies and the post office boys whose welfare, preferably in America or Australia, once loomed so large in his concerns. It seems most improbable that their contact survived the public end of the Cleveland Street affair. Like most working-class youths who find themselves suddenly spotlighted by involvement in a "case," Allies, Swinscow, Thickbroom, Newlove, and the rest faded — one assumes with great relief — from the sight of men who work with the written word. And historians, so dependent on what is printed and written for interpretation of the past, find the drama of such lives difficult to retrieve. Drama there must have been for working-class boys suddenly deprived of secure and honorable jobs and cast upon a cruelly competitive labor market without references and the undying stigma of a moral "offense" that could jeopardize their chances with even the most broad-minded employers. Our own researches have turned up some additional details on Allies and Thickbroom which seem to indicate that they managed to triumph over their early difficulties. Neither emigrated and both founded modest but upwardly mobile family dynasties. Their descendants, now established with secure niches in the great and accommodating English middle class, remember them with affection.

The characters who used their official positions to bring Cleveland Street into the open — those who did their simple duty — were noticeably less successful thereafter. JAMES MONRO, the Commissioner of the Metropolitan Police, survived in the post for less than two years. By the standards of the office it was exceptionally short and it is not difficult to see why. There is more than a suggestion in the memoranda on the Cleveland Street affair that Monro was lacking a proper awareness of his station and insufficiently grateful to his political superiors for his elevation to the top of the force. During the turbulent later months of 1880 when the dock laborers, gasworkers and coal-heavers came out on strike, the Tory press was sometimes bitterly critical of the role of the police — it was thought that they sometimes showed too much sympathy for the strike pickets who wanted to disrupt, and gave insufficient protection to the "blacklegs" brought in to undermine the strikers. By the summer of 1890, Monro found himself at the center of an industrial struggle in his own ranks in which his sympathies were firmly engaged on the side of the men. The police had long been petitioning for a superannuation scheme that would enable them to retire after twenty-five years with a pension. Monro supported this rank-and-file claim and was furious when the Tory Government turned it down. He was also angry about the maneuvering over a vacancy that arose for an Assistant Commissioner — Monro wanted to appoint a new Assistant from within the ranks, but the Home Office, which had powers of veto over the appointment, turned down his choices and urged that the job should go to one of their officials. Monro finally resigned in June 1890, expressing bitterness over the issues of superannuation and the appointments procedure.

But the Cleveland Street papers make it clear that there had been an underlying mood of bitterness throughout Monro's term, and, according to Labouchere, Monro threatened resignation because of the official obstacles to the investigation. Monro emerges as a crisp professional very much concerned with the integrity of his force. His letters are almost invariably brief and directly to the point. One senses that he understood the Establishment game but did not feel obliged to play it himself. To his superiors in the Home Office he may have looked very much like a man with a chip on his shoulder, and to the more intelligent members of the Tory administration, aware that the nascent signs of working-class consciousness were in some way inimical both to their own position and the cohesive myths of imperialism, James Monro must have seemed not quite the kind of person required to keep order at the heart of the empire. His resignation was accepted without any evidence of regret by the Home Secretary, Henry Matthews.

INSPECTOR FREDERICK ABBERLINE also appears to have suffered some loss of status. The whimpering end of the Cleveland Street affair was for him the postscript to two years of frustration. His record as one of Scotland Yard's ace detectives was by April 1890 overlaid by the image of the detective who failed to solve the Jack the Ripper murders and who had let Lord Arthur Somerset slip out of his grasp while in possession of immaculate evidence on the Cleveland Street case. Abberline's reputation never fully recovered.

SIR AUGUSTUS STEPHENSON, the Treasury Solicitor and Director of Public Prosecutions, had effectively served both the causes of disclosure and concealment. He had made it clear to those in authority who mattered that he was in fundamental disagreement with the handling of the case but, having lost the argument, made no attempt to communicate his dissatisfaction to the running dogs of exposure in Parliament and the press. He had expressed his view and that was enough. Sir Augustus continued to serve both as Treasury Solicitor and DPP until his retirement in 1894 when he had the satisfaction of handing on both posts to his able deputy.

THE HON. HAMILTON J. CUFFE served with distinction until 1908 when the functions of the Treasury Solicitor and the Public Prosecutor were split into two separate departments. Cuffe eventually succeeded to his brother's title and became the fifth Earl of Desart. He died in November 1934 at the age of eighty-six.

The journalistic investigators of the affair ended their professional careers less grandly than might have been predicted before Cleveland Street engaged their energies. ERNEST PARKE, the editor of *The North London Press*, remained a Radical hero, but almost withered away in prison. He was released from jail in July 1890, having served only six months of his one-year sentence, after a petition by journalists to the Home Office. He had lost fourteen pounds in weight but had acquired the (honorary) office of President of the Peckham and Dulwich Radical Club, an honor which may have seemed scant consolation for his time behind bars. In due course he became editor of *The Northern Echo* (like W. T. Stead), a respected member of the National Liberal Club, and, remarkable for a convicted person, a justice of the peace. He died, aged eighty-five, in 1944, consistent to the last — even in his posthumous papers he revealed no sources.

WILLIAM T. STEAD relinquished the editorship of *The Pall Mall Gazette* in 1890, moving on to higher and lower things. He founded several magazines, all short-lived; wrote a number of sensational and now forgotten books, including *If Christ Came to Chicago* (1893); and became increasingly obsessed by spiritualism. His sometime ally, Labouchere, wrote of him: "It is difficult to touch Pitch without being defiled . . . too much Purity has made him mad."

By 1899 Stead was convinced that he had inherited the spirit of Charles II. A friend noted that he had begun to confuse his own girl friends with the cavalier king's mistresses, endowing the ladies of the present with the attributes of these ghostly courtesans. Stead by now was campaigning for the adoption of one universal world religion, and also continuing the tradition of journalistic stunts which made him England's equivalent of William Randolph Hearst, although poorer. His speciality was the sensational and timely interview — "Chinese" Gordon, hero of the Sudan, and Viscount Wolseley, who had put down the Indian rising at the Red River in Canada, figured among his military scoops. After Stead had met him for a breakfast interview Wolseley wrote a mordant comment to his wife: "He [Stead] is the sort of man who in days of active revolution might be a serious danger. I looked at him thinking if it should ever be my lot to have to hang or shoot him."

Stead, never a sensitive man, went away thinking he had made an excellent impression. Wolseley's intuition that the sensation-mongering journalist was unlikely to die in bed proved more accurate than Stead's own assessments of the future, even with the help of the "spirit guides" he consulted ever more frequently in later life. In 1912 he was still casting round for headline-making stunts, and succeeded in convincing an editor that the first transatlantic crossing of the world's largest liner would make a series worthy of his personal touch. His news sense had not declined with age; the old instinct did not let him down, but the *Titanic* did. Stead went under with the ship "that could not sink."

HENRY LABOUCHERE was mildly disappointed when Gladstone passed him over for a Cabinet post when he formed his final administration in 1892, and his wife, the former actress Henrietta Hodson, was outraged when he was not given the Washington embassy as a consolation prize. (She actually lobbied everyone in sight behind his back; he wasn't keen on asking favors.) Gladstone, in fact, had pusillanimously avoided asking the Queen because, rightly no doubt, he assumed she would decline to accept one of her most hated critics.

Labby was no quitter; despite the ferocious intensity of his Cleveland Street campaign it was no more than another incident in his battle-scarred career. His ebullient energy was redirected, with scarcely a pause for breath, towards lobbying himself into a place on the parliamentary committee, whose function it was to vet royal expenditure. The new committee role was entirely to Labby's liking — almost at once he detected a characteristic example of what he regarded as Government chicanery. He found that estimates of the Queen's assets had made no allowance for the three enormous royal estates of Osborne, Sandringham, and Balmoral. Labby suggested she could provide for her numerous grandchildren by putting up one of these gargantuan properties for sale. The Government spokesman, mistaking his man, condescendingly explained that the estates and the great houses they contained were unsalable since no one could conceivably afford to buy them, let alone keep them up. This touched the Radical member's snobbery as well as his American-acquired republican sentiments; indeed he affected to find an affront to his own financial status and offered to write a cheque for £100,000 on the spot. This he reckoned was not only a fair price for Osborne, the sacred Italianate retreat on the Isle of Wight where the Queen spent most of her last years in range of Tennyson, the Poet Laureate, but also a sound investment.

The royal house, Labby thought, would serve very well as a sanitarium and the grounds, suitably parceled up into job lots, would be ideal for the kind of speculative cut-price construction that was becoming a late-nineteenth-century fashion. The suggestion was, of course, intentionally insulting; worse, Labouchere was perfectly capable of carrying it out.

Neither Labby nor his wife believed in God, but, after prolonged consideration, decided that their daughter Dora should be brought up as a Roman Catholic. The implication, as they privately admitted to each other, was that no one in England was good enough for her. In due course she was to marry two Italians; the first a prime minister, the second a prince.

The only honors he accepted were those of Privy Counsellor and an illuminated address from his Northampton constituents when he retired from Parliament at age sixty-nine in 1903. His last parliamentary campaign had been against the disastrous South African war which, courting the usual unanimous unpopularity, he had been the first important British political figure to condemn.

The last Labouchere anecdote finds him, in 1912, a fortnight away from death in his retirement villa in Florence, which had once belonged to Michelangelo. For the first time in his life he was ill enough to have stopped smoking the cheap cigarettes, twenty for a penny, which he always used. Someone upset an oil lamp causing a small fire in his bedroom. Awaking from sleep, Labby looked at the flames and remarked "Surely not so soon?"

LORD ARTHUR "PODGE" SOMERSET from the evening of October 18, 1889, when he fled the country became the subject of increasingly wild rumor and speculation. Like the Scarlet Pimpernel he was seen here, there, and "by those Frenchies" virtually everywhere. He had settled in Boulogne; he had shifted his quarters to Dieppe; he had moved on to Bucharest: he was in Constantinople. Here, according to the most reliable of contemporary reports, he presented himself at the corrupt court of Sultan Abdel Hamid II, but found the offer of his services as a military advisor rejected. There was, however, no question that whatever his specific whereabouts the former officer and confidant of the Prince of Wales generally found himself in a wretched situation.

In a sense he had got off lightly — he might have found himself breaking stones or in Reading Gaol; in another, the sentence he never served was left suspended over his head, a danger he could never forget. His punishment was, in effect, permanent exile, perhaps the heaviest borne by any of the participants. It was to last for thirty-six years.

By the end of 1890 he had finally settled in Hyeres, an old French Riviera resort, situated between Toulon and St. Raphael. There, at the Villa Sophie, he quietly lived out his days attended by a French cook and servants. He remained in communication with his family and some of his friends but never returned to England. The warrant for his arrest was never withdrawn. He died, aged seventy-four, on 26 May 1926 and was buried in the "English section" of the Hyeres town cemetery. The text on the headstone of his grave read: "The Memory of the Just is Blessed."

Sources and Bibliography

OFFICIAL PAPERS

The major source material stems from the files of the Director of Public Prosecutions kept at the Public Records Office, Chancery Lane, London. The Cleveland Street Dossier is No. DPP 1/95/1–7. The last two digits refer to seven envelopes, and these contain the following material.

ENVELOPE 1

Correspondence, 20 July 1889–11 August 1892.

ENVELOPE 2

Newspaper extracts, 12 September 1889–20 March 1890.

ENVELOPE 3

File 1. Opinions.
File 2. Opinion of Lord Chancellor.

File 3. Police report and statements.
File 4. Transcript of trial at Central Criminal Court of *R. v. Newlove and Veck.*
File 5. Sworn informations. *R. v. Newlove and Veck.*
File 6. Indictments. *R. v. Veck, Newlove, and Hammond.*

ENVELOPE 4

File 1. *R. v. Ernest Parke.*
File 2. *Re Saul.*

ENVELOPE 5

File 1. *R. v. Newton and Ors.* Chronological summary.
File 2. *R. v. Newton and Ors.* Correspondence.
File 3. *R. v. Newton and Ors.* Note of Till's statement re defense of Newton.
File 4. *Re Allies A. E.* Police report and three postal orders.
File 5. *Re Allies A. E.* Statement of Allies.
File 6. *Re Allies A. E.* Correspondence.

ENVELOPE 6

Papers *re* Labouchere.

ENVELOPE 7

File 1. "Flimsies," *i.e.*, duplicate copies, of certain letters.
File 2. Old envelopes.
File 3. Newspapers.

PRIVATE CASE BOOKS

These are kept under lock and key in the British Library.
Rose, Alfred. *Registrum Librorum Eroticorum.* London, 1936.

"Pisanus Fraxi" [H. S. Ashbee]. *Index Librorum Prohibitorum.* London, 1877.

———. *Centuria Librorum Absconditorum.* London, 1879.

———. *Catena Librorum Tacendorum.* London, 1885.

Saul, Jack. *Sins of the Cities of the Plain.* Privately printed, 1882.

BIOGRAPHIES, MEMOIRS, AND HISTORIES

Anonymous, *Kings, Courts and Society.* London: Jarrolds, 1921.

Benson, E. F. *As We Were: A Victorian Peep Show.* London: Longmans, 1930.

Bolitho, Hector, ed. *Further Letters on Queen Victoria.* London: Thornton Butterworth, 1938.

The Diary of Lady Fredrick Cavendish. 2 vols. London: John Murray, 1927.

Cowles, Virginia. *Edward VII and his Circle.* London: Hamish Hamilton, 1956.

Churchill, Sir Winston Spencer. *Lord Randolph Churchill.* London: Macmillan, 1906; Odhams, 1952.

Dilke, Charles. *Greater Britain.* London: Macmillan, 1868.

Engels, Friedrich. *The Condition of the Working Classes in England in 1884.* With preface written in 1892. London: Allen and Unwin.

Field, Julian Osgood. *Uncensored Recollections.* London: Eveleigh Nash, 1922.

Fulford, Roger. *The Prince Consort.* London: Macmillan, 1949.

Harris, Frank. *My Life and Loves.* London: W. H. Allen, 1964.

Harrison, Michael. *Clarence.* London: W. H. Allen, 1972.

Hyde, H. Montgomery. *Their Good Names.* London: Hamish Hamilton, 1970.

Houghton, Walter E. *The Victorian Frame of Mind.* New Haven: Yale University Press, 1957.

Langtry, Lillie. *The Days I Knew.* London: Hutchinson, 1925.

Lee, Sir Sidney. *Life of King Edward VII.* London: Macmillan, 1925.

Longford, Elizabeth. *Victoria R.I.* London: Weidenfeld and Nicholson, 1964.

Lustgarten, Edgar. *Verdict in Dispute.* London: Youth Book Club, 1950.

McCormick, Donald. *The Identity of Jack the Ripper.* London: Jarrolds, 1959.

Magnus, Sir Philip. *King Edward VII.* London: John Murray, 1964.

Mayhew, Henry. *London Labour and the London Poor.* 4 vols. London: Griffin, 1851–62.

Morris, James. *Pax Britannica*. London: Faber and Faber, 1968.

Pearsall, Ronald. *The Worm in the Bud*. London: Weidenfeld and Nicholson, 1969.

Pearson, Hesketh. *Labby, The Life of Henry Labouchere*. London: Hamish Hamilton, 1936.

Ponsonby, Sir Frederick. *Recollections of Three Reigns*. London: Eyre and Spottiswoode, 1951.

Rees, J. D. *The Duke of Clarence and Avondale in India*. London: Kegan Paul Trench Trubner, 1891.

Russell, Bertrand, ed. *Ideas and Beliefs of the Victorians*. London: Sylvan Press, 1949.

Stephen, J. K. *Quo Musa Tendis*. Cambridge: Bowes and Macmillan, 1888.

————. *Lapsus Calami*. Cambridge: Bowes and Macmillan, 1896.

Strachey, Lytton. *Queen Victoria*. London: Chatto and Windus, 1921.

————. *Eminent Victorians*. London: Chatto and Windus, 1918.

Trevelyan, G. M. *British History in the Nineteenth Century*. London: Longmans Green, 1922.

Tingsten, Herbert. *Victoria and the Victorians*. Translated from the Swedish *Viktoria Och Viktorianerna* by D. Grey and E. L. Grey. London: Allen and Unwin, 1972.

Vincent, James. *HRH The Duke of Clarence*. London: John Murray, 1893. (Official memoir.)

PERIODICALS, JOURNALS, AND NEWSPAPERS

The Daily Telegraph

The Field

The Graphic

Lloyds Sunday Newspaper

The Morning Post

The North London Press

The Pall Mall Gazette

The Penny Illustrated Newspaper

The Police Gazette

The Queen

Reynolds's Newspaper

The Saturday Review

The Scottish Leader

The Times

Truth

Vanity Fair

Westminster Review

Woman

Yellow Book